Land Whisperer

a guide to partnering energetically with any environment

Carol Rosenblum Perry

Also by Carol Rosenblum Perry

The Fine Art of Technical Writing
(1991; revised 2011)

Contents

**For
Henni Luria**

*who, at age 5, told us
"People are the eyes and ears of the Earth."*

VI
Rationalists, wearing square hats,
Think, in square rooms,
Looking at the floor,
Looking at the ceiling.
They confine themselves
To right-angled triangles.
If they tried rhomboids,
Cones, waving lines, ellipses —
As, for example, the ellipse of the half moon —
Rationalists would wear sombreros.

— Wallace Stevens,
"Six Significant Landscapes"
The Collected Poems of Wallace Stevens,
1982, Random House NY

Note To Readers

The stories recounted in this book are drawn from my land-whispering practice. To protect confidentiality for my human clients, I omit names and may slightly alter content but *only* to mask location or other identifiers. Apart from that, *these are actual experiences.* Nothing has been embellished or fabricated.

We don't have good language for the practice described in this book for two reasons. First, *language reflects culture.* Concepts absent from a culture will be absent from, or poorly articulated by, its language(s). Second, *language is dimensional.* Language is a product of the 3rd dimension (3D); using words to describe non-3D experiences is paradoxical. With enough energy behind them, however, words can be jump-off points for our awareness, opening doors to places words themselves cannot go. As Don Juan explains to Carlos in Carlos Castaneda's *The Active Side of Infinity* (1998, HarperCollins NY): "Language is inadequate. All these experiences are beyond syntax."

What's A Land Whisperer Anyway?

"…the healers Lokesh had trained with believe the health of the land and the health of the people who inhabited it were inextricably linked…it was impossible to treat a human illness without addressing the state of harmony in the human's spirit, and it was impossible to address the harmony in a human spirit without also considering the harmony in that part of the earth where the human lived…"

— from *Bone Mountain*, Eliot Pattison, 2002,
St. Martin's Press, NY

THE SEED FOR THIS BOOK was sown in June 2012 a day after I met with a family about their newly purchased acreage. They were early in the process of getting to know their land and seeking informal guidance. Later on, I realized, they might want to hire my services as a land whisperer.[1]

What I call land whispering or land work is *the shamanic practice of partnering energetically with a given environment to assure or restore balance.* In this context, the land is a complex comprising all lifeforms, elements, and structures upon, within, or above a piece of ground of any size and usage. This is true whether the environment is wilderness, managed farmland, a suburban neighborhood, a forest, an ocean, or a commercial center in a large city. Think of the land complex as a container of energy, form, relationship, and interaction.

The practice draws upon fundamental knowledge about how the world works — that is, how the world works beyond the level most of us engage with every day: beyond personal and cultural programming and a materially based worldview.

As a land whisperer I conduct the work in collaboration with an interdimensional team comprising a core group and members associated with each specific site and situation. Much of what we do centers on clearing patterns of disharmony held within the environment, sometimes for long periods, and resetting a fresh energetic baseline that frees the land complex to attract to it a more balanced set of behaviors and patterns and, in effect, redirect its storyline. Other aspects of the work include helping souls transition and conducting soul retrieval for the land itself in areas devastated by violence or other trauma. Whatever the situational specifics, the key to a successful land-human partnership is a land worker's ability to communicate via subtle energy — this is the essence of "whispering."

---

[1] Terms that may not be familiar, especially if this is new territory for you, may be explained further in appropriate text sections and also make up the Glossary.

Land whispering may be done proactively or reactively, and in either case the land initiates the process through a call, which lines up the right person for the right job at the right time. Proactive work helps avoid creating imbalances, or what humans perceive as problems. Reactive work deals with existing imbalances, many of which developed because no person was aware enough to be proactive in the first place.

So, for example, if you intend to prepare a site for development, it's wise to proactively consult the land while you're formulating plans to excavate, locate structures or roadways, move stones, reconfigure waterways, or alter gradients. You may need to modify your original plans or process to accommodate the land. Proactive work also includes preparing property for sale, to address issues beyond market forces and attract a more conscious buyer; readying property for rent, to attract a more conscious tenant; and maintaining public and business spaces, to support smoother interactions, promote a more comfortable, productive environment, and, in the case of retail businesses, improve customer relations and sales. Think of proactive maintenance as a good energetic "spring cleaning."

But if a series of businesses fail, one after another, on a commercial property you own, for example, reactive work would be called for, as it would be if a downtown is stagnating or dying, crop areas are unproductive or disease ridden despite proper care, or a home, business, neighborhood, or public venue repeatedly attracts conflict or violence. Reactive work also includes helping the land rebalance after Nature-based events such as hurricanes, earthquakes, volcanic eruptions, flooding, tsunamis, tornadoes, and severe electrical storms as well as from human-caused events such as wars, toxic spills, and terrorism.

The family I met with in 2012 spent about an hour with me, and that brief interaction energized me in an unexpected way. The following day, inspiration overtook me without warning in the midst of lunch and I found myself simultaneously eating and scribbling the chapter headings of a book I hadn't known I was about to start writing. This came unbidden, as calls tend to do.

This book reintroduces readers to the land-human partnership, our oldest partnership on Earth, and clarifies our place within the partnership and our responsibility to it. It shows how the land-human partnership is a *living, interactive, energetic relationship* and how to actually *conduct that relationship*.

The book can be read on several interlinked levels: as educational information, as basic training for prospective practitioners, as a guide to an awareness practice, or as some or all of the preceding. And although it presents a pragmatic approach, a way of working, it's not about technique. It's about a way of being in the world, a way of sensing and understanding; it's about a part of our human inheritance many of us have disconnected from and would be wise to reclaim.

Many people today would dismiss land whispering and its foundations outright as fantastical, far-fetched, or simply impossible. I might have once too. But direct experience opened a doorway, showing me something deeper, truer, transformative, and inviting me to participate. You have that opportunity as well, but it may require putting aside old beliefs.

Herein I offer up concepts, processes, protocols, and stories. The journey thereafter is yours.

THE LAND–HUMAN PARTNERSHIP

"…The ancient gods of the Maori…had not given unto man their bounty without strictures. Everything was connected. Man had a reciprocal responsibility to the world. There was a cycle of birth, death, and replenishment which had to be maintained. There was also an implicit contract with the soil, with all things animate and inanimate, that had to be respected and honored. It was not a contract given either to abuse or to play with…the relationship was not something about which either had a choice…Man, be not respecting the contract, was in danger of killing both his world and himself…"

— Rongo Mahana reflecting as he planted his fields, from *Whanau II*, by Witi Ihimaera, 2004, Reed Publishing, Auckland, NZ

Nature Of The Partnership

Humans have an inherent partnership with the land. This is not a metaphor. The partnership is our oldest, and primary, relationship, dating from our earliest days on Earth. Indigenous peoples the world over recognize the partnership, though some no longer live it. But whether recognized or not, adhered to or not, the partnership remains vibrant. In fact, I'd say the land is reasserting itself as an active partner *with attitude*. If you doubt this, just look around the planet and consider Nature's increasingly extreme behavior.

Many of us have been raised and continue to live in cultures whose approach to land is one of "dominion over." Too often, we treat land as a commodity, failing to consider what *the land itself* requires to remain in or return to a state of balance. Even many people who don't view land as a commodity, who are environmentally sensitive and seek sustainable ways to live, superimpose their designs on the land. But when you approach the land as a partner and consult it, as you would any partner, about its own needs and preferences, your relationship with the land shifts dramatically — and so do outcomes.

Like any partnership, ours with the land involves agreements whose bedrock is as follows:

- *The land is sovereign.* You may hold legal title to property, but you don't own the land. No one does. Your role is as *steward*. This is both a privilege and a responsibility. Stewardship requires a high level of integrity, excellent communication skills, the willingness to compromise, and an affinity for teamwork — all of which are addressed throughout this book.

- *The land is self-sustaining.* Species come and go, continents drift, glaciers migrate. Yet the land endures in one form or another on micro and macro scales. It has done so for thousands of millennia, and there's no indication that's about to change. The land as "self-sustaining" is different from what we refer to nowadays as "sustainability" — that is, the human-centered need to support planetary resources and systems to assure our own survival. The cold reality is this: *though humans cannot sustain themselves without reference to the land, the land can sustain itself without reference to humans and, some might say, would be better off without us.*

- *The land is healed co-creatively.* Nature has agreed to absorb and hold toxic energies resulting from human actions, especially violence, even though this undermines balance for the period such energies are held, and humans have agreed to help transmute those energies — that is, help shift them from one level to another — to restore balance. In this way, the partners share responsibility (*Universal Light Series 2*, Perelandra Center for Nature Research, 1985).

- *The land must be shown respect.* Every partnership is founded upon the cornerstone of *respect*, and it's no different with land and humans. Many of the problems revealed through land whispering have, at their core, issues of disrespect. When you show the land respect through your intentions, words, and actions — these must be aligned! — it responds accordingly. Where there's a lack of respect, the land may acquiesce for the time being, but sooner or later there will be consequences, their intensity commensurate with the level of disrespect shown. If the situation is serious and ongoing, and you fail to put things right, the powers that be will terminate your stewardship privileges through co-creatively arranged shifts in your life circumstances: a sudden move for a job, a family situation propelling you elsewhere, a change in your finances. Given enough time, Nature always has the last word.

Disrespect is rarely deliberate, more often the product of our tendency towards mindlessness or the limits of our awareness, as the following two personal stories illustrate.

Neglecting the Social Courtesies

WHEN DAVID AND I ARRIVED in Hawai'i on his university sabbatical, we were so excited to be there that we forgot our manners, failing at the outset to introduce ourselves to the spirits of place. We'd rented a sweet house at the edge of a woods where the remains of an old Hawaiian community were evident. That in itself should have signaled us, but, as I say, we were distracted by the delights of our new island lifestyle.

Over the first several weeks, a heavy wooden sliding closet door fell off its track, the dishwasher overflowed, and the oven timer sounded loudly more than once in the middle of the night. Taken independently, each of these episodes was trivial and meaningless. Taken together, however, they formed a pattern and sent a message. Those rascally energies I call gremlins had started "misbehaving" to attract our attention because something was amiss. Once we got the message, we redressed the issue: standing at the edge of the woods, we greeted the place, introduced ourselves to its many resident lifeforms, and expressed our peaceful intentions. Immediately, gremlin activity ceased and never recurred. ✦

OVERLOOKING THE MICROSCOPIC

I'D BEEN SICK FOR SEVERAL WEEKS with a persistent virus that had drained me of vitality, and I was having a hard time recovering. Then, one night, I had a dream in which I saw the virus. I just *knew* this is what the image represented. I was struck by its white, lacy beauty and its ingenious reproductive intelligence: a small piece of "lace" would break off and become the starter for another virus in a kind of viral "vegetative propagation."

Upon reflection, the dream's purpose was equally clear: the virus was demanding my respect. I had been so intent on getting rid of it that I'd failed to honor it. Yes, *honor*! Land whispering has taught me to view lifeforms we humans have prejudices against — those that make us ill, those we consider pests or have phobias about, those we see (judge) as gross or ugly — in a different light. So I thanked the virus for the lesson (the dream) and whatever other purposes it may have served and kindly asked it to leave. It did in short order. Granted, it would have left eventually. But I sensed it did so sooner *and on a different basis* once I accorded it the proper respect. ←

THE LAND'S STORY

Each piece of land resides within the context of its geologic, climatic, ecological, and human history. This is the land's individual story. But that story falls within the much larger context of the surrounding land mass (or ocean). And because physical borders are artificial constructs based on politics or culture, and because energy isn't bounded in the way that matter is, every individual story bears upon all others and, ultimately, the planet as a whole and beyond.

Within a story's human history is the aggregate of culture over time — ethnicity, race, religion and spirituality, governance and war, technology, commerce, agriculture and natural resource use, the arts, social customs and practice, ethics — and the complexity of that history continues to revise the story's narrative. Most heavily affected are places where conflict has persisted for long periods and where outsiders' hunger for power has shattered indigenous ways of life. It is crucial to remember *we all were indigenous once* and still carry deep within us the universal experience of being born of the land as well as an ancestral connection to a particular place no matter how "dis-placed" we are now.

People who still live where their ancestors lived for generations have a multilevel relationship with the land and detailed knowledge extending to individual trees, stones, mountains, water sources, and other natural features and power centers. These features may have names and be known personally. Such a set of relationships defines who the people are as individuals, as families, and as a community in a way many of us now "dis-placed" have forgotten. If ancestral lands are destroyed or the group is forced to move away, as has often been the case with first nations, the people suffer a communal grief many never recover from. The impact is multigenerational. For in losing their land they lose their cultural identity and the source of their well-being, and in losing those they lose their soul — a loss held not only in the genetic and energetic inheritance of the human descendants but also by the land itself even after those who experienced it directly are long gone. Thus disheartened, the land may decline and lose its soul as well.

Many of us in the modern world are no longer anchored to place in this land-born way. We move around a lot, and our familiarity with a given place is superficial unless we have the awareness and take the time to get to know it. Implicit in this is understanding *each place has a spirit*, and *that spirit links to far more than we can perceive with our five physical senses*. Whether we realize it consciously or not, humans both alter, and are altered by, the land's evolving story. And it is this evolving story that is at the heart of land whispering.

Communicating With The Land

"…In the oldest religion, everything was alive, not super-naturally but naturally alive. There were only deeper and deeper streams of life, vibrations of life more and more vast.…For the whole life-effort of man was to get his life into direct contact with the elemental life of the cosmos, mountain-life, cloud-life, thunder-life, air-life, earth-life, sun-life. To come into immediate felt contact, and so derive energy, power, and a dark sort of joy…"

— D.H. Lawrence, talking about the
Pueblo Indians, from *The Spell of New Mexico*,
edited by Tony Hillerman, 1976, University of
New Mexico Press, Albuquerque

A S WITH EVERY PARTNERSHIP, communications are crucial. So just how do you communicate with the land? Or, put another way, how do you come into "immediate *felt* contact," as D.H. Lawrence calls it, with the land?

The key is working with subtle energy.

THE (VERY) SUBTLE WORLD

Stories of how the universe began, from the mythic to what contemporary science calls the Big Bang, have in common the element of *vibration*. What distinguishes one vibration from another is its *frequency* (a temporal measure) and its *wavelength* (a spatial measure).

One way to understand the beginning is this: The first vibration, however characterized, differentiated first from the One, the Void, the Unknowable, and that event was the first in a process of differentiation that is ongoing to this day. Thus a great family of vibrations was born and continues to evolve. And we who came relatively late in the differentiation process now call the great family of vibrations *Nature* or the *Universe* or the *World*, and the vibrating substrate *subtle energy*.

Perceiving the world as energy

The world is *as we perceive it to be*.

Humans have two basic ways of perceiving the world, though in practice the two interact and we use them as a package.

We perceive matter through the familiar five physical senses: sight, hearing, smell, taste, and touch. Yet the world of matter is just one particular set of vibrations to which we're strongly attuned. Whether conscious of it or not, we also perceive the world as subtle energy through more refined, differently oriented senses, our subtle senses, which allow us to interact with realities beyond the material. It's our subtle senses we rely on most with the land-human partnership because *communications within the partnership are energetic.*

Subtle energy may be perceived as a gentle tingling, a sensation of heat or cold apart from physical temperature, a faint tone unrelated to physical hearing, a light or color apart from physical seeing, a feeling ("gut reaction"), an image (often symbolic), or an intuition (knowing without conscious thought).

For instance, when first coming onto a site for land whispering, I may sense the land's response to my presence as an overall feeling: a comfortable feeling means "Come in, you're welcome, let's get to know one another"; an uncomfortable feeling, "Do not enter at this time" or, more strongly, "Do not enter...period." I've also experienced being welcomed initially and then sensing a sudden shift, knowing I no longer belong there for whatever reason and need to leave immediately. I take these feelings seriously, don't second-guess them, and don't engage my intellect.

What's key about perceiving energy is that it *encodes information.* So by learning to "read" energy — that is, to perceive it and interpret those perceptions — you gain a larger understanding of the world; enhance your ability to alter your responses to and behavior in the world; experience directly the interconnectedness, kinship, and conscious nature of all life; and, through the preceding, expand your awareness.

Reading energy

Humans are born with the innate ability to read energy, an ability that, like so many others, can be honed into a highly prized skill through practice. And because reading energy relies on signs, symbols, and nuanced cues — the subtle world can be *very* subtle — interpretation is crucial. In a given situation, there may be several reasonable interpretations of the energetic "raw data" you perceive. So how do you know if what you've interpreted is correct?

Discernment, the finely balanced marriage of sensing and thinking, is what allows you to interpret your perceptions with the greatest degree of accuracy. It's developed through experience, practice, and trust in your guidance (higher level wisdom). It also is what allows you to distinguish the land's true voice from other voices you may perceive, as well as from your own internally generated emotions, habitual beliefs, and programmed agendas.

Discernment involves a working partnership between what I call the sensing body (intuition) and the thinking body (intellect). This is just a way of talking, a model to aid understanding: these are two intertwined aspects of consciousness, not discrete entities.

The sensing body is the part of you that resonates with truth or falsehood. It interpenetrates your whole system, and you connect with it through feelings and other bodily responses. For instance, when someone lies to you, how can you tell? Through a fluttering in the pit of your stomach? A constriction in your throat? A ripple along your spine? General discomfort or unease? Some part of you senses that *the words spoken don't match the energy behind them*. You may not be able to explain your response rationally, nor do you need to: you just *know*. The sensing body is an invaluable barometer not only for land whispering but also for larger level energywork (see "When Land Work Is *Earth Work*").

The thinking body is the part of you that crunches data to assemble mental constructs that can be created or destroyed at will: beliefs, assumptions, analyses, theories, classifications, and the like. The thinking body appears to source from the brain, and its unique capabilities appear to distinguish humans from other lifeforms. I twice say "appear" because these understandings are themselves beliefs. The intellect is a marvelous faculty when used appropriately, and essential for certain aspects of land whispering. But when given free rein, it tends toward arrogance and self-promotion. *Believing* is not *knowing*.

Reading energy also involves intuitive mirroring (divination). Your intuition seeks an external "screen" upon which to project information (messages) you already hold but haven't accessed consciously. Some people use formal systems such as tarot and other card decks, I Ching, runes, and palmistry as their mirror. Absent those, or in combination with them, the Universe uses whatever's handy so you "get the message."

Messages can come from any source, and messengers take myriad forms. Important messages often are delivered through dreams, signs from the natural world, or "accidents."[2] But they also come from the more prosaic. For instance, the next time your car breaks down, take a closer look at what has occurred and use it as intuitive mirroring. Is the problem a faulty battery (power issue), ignition (getting started, initiating action), or braking (living without adequate self-control), and so on. When viewed symbolically, the specific problem may tell you something your auto mechanic certainly can't! Every aspect of the message and messenger signifies. It's all part of the "read."

Over time, you'll develop a unique lexicon of signs and symbols that help with the read. For instance, color can be informative. I associate golden energy with purification, red with heat, blue with coolness and calm. That said, there are times when these associations *don't* apply, which I suss out through discernment. I associate green with *either* loving *or* toxic energy — two opposing poles[3] — and interpretation depends on discerning the larger context and reading the situation more deeply.

The natural world often provides guidance. For instance, when a guardian spirit appears in a certain physical form, I take it as a heads-up to pay close attention and proceed with caution, knowing that further information awaits me and will bear strongly on how I go forward.

---

[2] What we call *accidents* in the material world are *synchronicities* in the subtle world. That is, there are deeper, hidden connections between seemingly random events.

[3] These opposing poles make sense *alchemically*, as "turning poison into medicine" is a healer's ultimate task.

Likewise, a particular power animal moving in a particular way signals whether I am heading in the right direction or am off-track and in what way; if that animal sits still, I know to wait and to defer action.

My set of indicators works for me. Yours may be quite different yet just as effective.

Reading energy is not a parlor trick — it's a responsibility. You must be clear and your intentions beyond reproach. Imposing your personal will upon a situation is arrogant and potentially dangerous to you and others. For more a detailed discussion, see "Ethics" and "Caveats" in "Land Whispering As A Path."

Tips for working with subtle energy

The following tips will get you off to a good start, not just with land whispering but with any intuitive practice. The rest you'll learn over time by doing.

- *Be attentive to all "blips" coming across your intuitive radar screen.* Subtle energy is just that: *subtle.* The little blips we tend to dismiss as "nothing" may very well be "something" and may hold the key to interpreting the read.

- *Keep your intellect out of the process when reading energy.* If you find yourself judging or analyzing what you perceive, your intellect's interfering. The intellect has an important role to play later on, after you've received the raw data and need to interpret it (discernment). Don't fall for the inner voice that insists "It's just your imagination" or "You're making this up." You may be surprised how persistent that voice can be.

- *Formulate questions with yes-or-no answers, especially when you're first learning.* The yes-or-no format helps you sense the accuracy of the information you receive and builds your intuitive skills for perceiving more complex responses. Kinesiology, also known as muscle testing, a technique you may want to incorporate into your process later on, requires the yes-or-no format for asking questions.

- *Take the first thing you get.* Information may arrive so quickly you question its veracity or your own skills. Don't doubt, then second-guess — that's the intellect interfering again — or you'll muddy your read.

- *Trust what you get.* This is a big one! Trust and doubt cannot co-exist.

- *Journal what you get.* Details fade or disappear entirely over time. And details can be significant, especially when you're doing repeat work on the same land. Moreover, additional related data may arrive later, sometimes *much* later (weeks, months, even years). So retain all the pieces — and you may not know what "all the pieces" are except *in hindsight*.

ALL OUR RELATIONS

Many tribal people refer to the great web of life as "all our relations," and *these relations are a land whisperer's communicants.* When someone calls a non-human lifeform "sister" or "brother," "aunty" or "uncle," "grandmother" or "grandfather," it is meant literally, and that relative, that family member, is treated with love, appreciation, and respect. At the start of my practice I knew intellectually that we're all related: after all, we source from the same beginning and thus are made of the same material and energetic stuff. But it wasn't until I started land whispering that I *felt* this and could begin to act on that felt knowledge. You may need to allow yourself the time to *feel* this larger familial connection as well.

It follows, then, that all our relations are *animate*. This too may require an adjustment on your part as your intellect continues to insist this cannot be the case. I've learned, for example, that stones are not inanimate, not inert chunks of matter: they're alive! This is neither a belief nor a romanticized notion about Nature, but something I now experience directly.

Human-made constructions are animate too and could be construed as one of our many relations, albeit of a different order. I realize this may be a stretch. But think about it. They're crafted from materials that source from the Earth (e.g., wood, mineral ores); the materials' manufacturing processes involve natural elements and forces (e.g., fire, water, electricity); and the final products are infused with their designers' and builders' creative and physical energies. Beyond this, constructions take on a life of their own — a spirit, a presence, an essence, call it what you like: a feeling that cannot quite be accounted for but cannot be denied.

All our relations communicate, and they do so *energetically* — which is why perceiving and reading subtle energy are key to this practice. You may at first be surprised at the breadth of the land's demographics and, even more so, at what some of your relations have to say.

The biosphere

Whether feral or domesticated, wild or cultivated, all biologically based lifeforms communicate. During the process of land whispering, nonhuman animals, insects, plants, microbes, and others can indicate a problem, contribute information to the deeper assessment, and even confirm through their behavior *after* the work has completed that the problem has been solved (or not).

For example, one client's dogs were so traumatized by an earthquake that they were having difficulty recovering. But after the energies of both the earthquake itself and the resulting trauma were cleared from the property and the land rebalanced, all the dogs, even the most sensitive, became playful again. In another instance, an energetically aggressive human neighbor induced fear in a client's sheep and horses by his mere presence along the property line; the animals retreated from the affected area, where they normally grazed, and the sheep were so intimidated they wouldn't go anywhere without the horses. Once the land was cleared of the aggression and a protective energetic barrier put in place, the animals calmed down, reclaimed their space, and acted normal again. In both cases, the animals were part of the call *and* signposts of resolution.

Serious gardeners know the land responds to their ministrations in tangible ways. Devoting more attention to plants and soil not only by watering, fertilizing, and mulching but also by *being present in a respectful and caring manner* creates greater well-being for all on multiple levels. Some of the effects are gross, for instance, increased fruiting and flowering. Others are subtle, more a sensation, a vibration. When I lived in Hawai'i, the plants at our place preferred macadamia nut husks as mulch above every other kind of mulch material. When those husks were spread on beds and under fruit trees, I could almost hear the plants aspirating "Ahhhh…"

Dogs, cats, horses, certain birds, and other animals bred over time to be companions to humans provide a perfect opportunity for learning how to communicate with other species. Because companion animals live partly in the human world, we have more overlap and concentrated interaction, and the animals' cues are easier to read. But the *communications process is the same* with lifeforms less closely connected to us, including those we have preconceptions about or even biases against, as the following small stories reflect.

The Sociable Wasp

ONE WINTER IN OREGON, a solitary wasp overwintered inside a recessed light fixture in our kitchen. At dinnertime, the wasp came out and joined us at the counter while we ate. We never knew exactly what drew it out at that time of day: artificial light, warmth, food smells, something about its natural biorhythm, something more purely vibrational, or some combination of these? The wasp wasn't aggressive; it just hung around us, as if enjoying the company. When dinner was over, it flew back to its hideaway. Although I didn't consciously communicate with the wasp then — I didn't have the awareness — in hindsight it's clear there must have been communication going on: we three established a safe, comfortable, consistent pattern. A wasp and humans interacting socially — who knew?! ↢

The Agreeable Roaches

A FRIEND OF MINE TELLS A STORY about her favorite uncle, who lived for years in New York City. Like many apartment buildings, his was periodically treated to exterminate roaches. But Uncle had an agreement with the roaches — yes, you heard me! — and they never became a problem in his apartment. I wasn't privy to the details so can only speculate on how this worked. My guess: the roaches agreed to keep their numbers down in exchange for a certain consideration on Uncle's part. When the exterminators came to do their job, they learned to skip his apartment. No roaches gone wild, no need for treatment. ↢

RATS WITH ATTITUDE

WHEN LIVING IN RURAL HAWAI'I, I tried to create an agreement with rats, *tried* being the operative word. Rats abound in the woods and like to shelter in structures, now and then finding their way into attics or outbuildings. They can cause a variety of problems indoors, and where there are two rats there will soon be more. We used to set traps when hearing "visitors upstairs"; we'd catch one or two, and things would quiet for a time. But I never liked the trapping and killing. I just wanted these particular relations out of the house.

In my communications with them, I greeted the rats respectfully, apologized for the trapping, told them I meant them no harm, reminded them they had the whole outdoors, and offered them the use of the garden shed rather than the house if they were seeking an indoor space. But some relations are not naturally receptive or inclined to be compliant, and rats are a good case in point: they are bold, fearless, and smart, and they reproduce so rapidly that losses to traps seem to concern them not at all. In our communiqués, they displayed what I can only call "attitude": "We are rats…we can do what we like…we'll take your request under advisement." I had modest success, perhaps because I showed respect and a willingness to at least *ask*. But every now and then I still heard visitors upstairs, just to remind me I didn't have dominion, and that rat-in-residence sound was my cue to ask again. ✦

FELINE INSTANT MESSAGING

WHEN OUR CAT BONNIE WAS YOUNG, she'd periodically go adventuring and be away for days, even weeks. We never figured out where she went or why, and she always returned, hungry but (except in one instance) no less the worse for wear.

Over time, she and I developed a communications protocol that helped me (and perhaps her?) during her absences, a kind of human-feline instant messaging. I'd connect with her energetically and she'd send me a picture — one of what came to be a small set of symbolic icons I learned to read. If she was on her way home, I'd see an image of her trotting along briskly; that meant she'd be back "soon." But if I saw her sitting still, the tradewinds ruffling her fluffy fur, I knew she'd be gone for "a while." I never tried to quantify what "soon" or "a while" meant. Every now and then, there'd be an anomalous image, not from the established icon set, and I'd interpret that as best I could. Sometimes I'd just ask, "Are you okay?" and her response came across as a feeling.

I also used this protocol to keep in touch with Bonnie when I traveled — that is, when it was *my* absence, not hers — and to reassure her I'd be back.

The one time Bonnie was *not* okay while away, she sent me a powerful message through a dream: she led me from our house to a hole in the ground, then immediately went down the hole and disappeared. I knew I could not follow. Upon waking, I was very upset, sure she had died and this was her way of telling me. Weeks passed and no Bonnie, and we had begun to accept and grieve the loss. Then late one afternoon as we were unpacking the car from a day at the beach, there she was in the driveway near the house! She was a wreck: skinny, her fur chewed and patchy, her smell not right. I don't know what kind of difficulties she encountered going down "the hole in the ground" but she must have come close to dying and it took weeks of healing work to bring her back to a state of well-being. ✦

Amazing Grace

WHEN NEWCOMERS TO HAWAI'I, we lived on the slopes of the dormant volcano Hualalai in North Kona in a sweet rental house adjacent to a woods. It was quiet and private — just our style.

During a period when David was on the US mainland, a small spider appeared on the lanai and spun a correspondingly small web in one corner. I didn't pay much attention at first. But as the days went by, she remained and grew, as did her web. We co-existed peaceably, and when David returned I introduced him to my spider companion, now firmly ensconced.

One day I had a notion to touch her; that is, I suddenly wanted to touch her and thought she would allow it. With hindsight, I'd say she *asked me* to do this. So I approached her gingerly and slowly extended my index finger toward one of her front legs. She didn't move. My fingertip made contact with the leg and I began to stroke it. She didn't move at first, then delicately stretched the leg out a little farther as if to encourage me. She seemed mesmerized by my touch. I know animals may freeze when afraid or to avoid detection, but this had a very different feeling. It wasn't paralysis. She was zoned. I was amazed by the interaction — thus her name Amazing Grace.

After a while, Grace relocated to one side of the entryway to the lanai. By then she was an expert weaver with a large, complex, and productive web. However, her new location made it difficult for us to enter and exit the lanai without disturbing or, worse, destroying the web. Not sure what to do, we discussed the issue one afternoon while standing beside her on her web.

Early the next morning, we were astonished to discover that *the web had been moved to the other side of the entryway, where it was no longer in harm's way!* Yesterday's web had been deconstructed — not a shred of it remained — and a complete, new structure spun in the new safer location overnight.

Think what you like, but we could only conclude that Grace had "heard" and "understood" our discussion and acted on it. ❖

Coral on the Move

A LANDOWNER EMAILED ME about a perplexing situation in the labyrinth she had built with guidance from a friend who also had built a labyrinth on her own property. Somehow the "stones" (actually pieces of coral) that formed the labyrinth had been dislodged from their original placements. And not just a few pieces, but most of them. The owner assured me she had followed the proper protocols for gathering, so lack of permission wasn't at issue. She and her husband had concluded wild pigs were not responsible for the disturbance — the pattern didn't fit — and they were unaware of, and couldn't imagine, any person coming on site and maliciously or even mischievously moving the coral around.

At the labyrinth, in a shady grove uphill from the house, I walked around solo. The coral was indeed in disarray, the once smoothly contoured arcs disfigured and coral pieces scattered this way and that. The owner told me this was her special personal place before she built the labyrinth there: she and this place were deeply connected. She also told me she'd been going through issues of her own right before the disturbance in the labyrinth and was perceptive enough to acknowledge that her own chaos was being mirrored by the corals' disarray.

But the strong hit I got was entirely different: The coral was on the move! That is, the coral wanted the labyrinth to be moved, though when I asked where to, there was silence. I concluded that was for the owner to discern, not me or my team. What might have appeared to be the "perfect spot" for the labyrinth from a human perspective might not have been from the land's, or more specifically, the corals'. Or the siting might have been fine at first but, for whatever reason, wasn't any longer.

I did the only thing I could at that point: encouraged the owner to sit in the middle of the labyrinth — her special place — ask questions, then listen carefully for the answers. ❦

The elements

Fire, water, earth, and air — the four elements — all participate in land whispering on multiple levels: the physical, medicinal, environmental, cosmological, archetypal, astrological, purely energetic. Of the four, I've partnered most with water and sometimes on a large scale (see "When Land Work Is *Earth* Work"), but all the elements can be lively communicants on any scale as the following examples illustrate.

In my early days as a land whisperer I was called to a condominium unit in a multi-unit building that was part of a golf-course community in south Florida. The current owner was experiencing nightmares and sudden strange shifts in some of her behavior. The condo had previously been confiscated by the authorities because of drug dealing, and there had been a suspicious death in the unit above, either a suicide or drug overdose. This history in itself indicated the need for clearing.

But there was more, a second layer that also begged for redress: persistent plumbing problems and an as yet undiagnosed disharmony involving the pond behind the multi-unit building. This pond was part of the water-management system serving the golf-course community. The plumbing and pond situations indicated water issues and before setting up the clearing I invited in a team to investigate further.

We quickly learned that the spirit of water in the pond was unhappy. I sensed energetic stagnation around the pond and had the feeling the pond needed to be outletted in a different way, whether physically, energetically, or both wasn't clear. In any event, there was a problem with *flow*, which by its nature links to water. The big egret frequenting the canal near the pond sounded off, disgruntled about the impact of humans on his environment. Ah, there it was! The core message: disrespect. So in addition to clearing the energetic imprints from the condo's dodgy history, my team and I worked with water's discontent around human manipulation to help repair the relationship and, I hoped, create greater awareness and better communications within the land-human partnership…and put an end to plumbing problems.

Sometimes more than one element needs attention to assure balance. For instance, too much fire and not enough water or earth may indicate too much male energy and not enough female energy, although this is not the only possible interpretation (see "Male and Female Energies" in "Spirit Nation: the Unseen Ones").

One property I worked with had a water/earth imbalance below ground, concentrated at the base of the steep hillside behind the house. I perceived an underground "flow of stones" and something about that flow was blocked, amping up energy in a harmful way. It was as if the house was sitting on "too much water," although there wasn't an obvious physical drainage problem, and the water and earth elements had become conflated. To resolve this, I asked that any blockages in that area be released so that energy could flow smoothly and freely, knowing this would naturally relieve the enmeshment of water and earth and rebalance them. If there was a drainage problem that could be remedied physically, it would still be important to resolve any underlying energetic issues, otherwise those would manifest again in a new physical form.

On another property I sensed strongly male and female areas (over 10 acres) that were reinforced by energetic transects to two large mountains, one more fiery and earthy, the other more watery. It may seem strange to speak of mountains this way, but remember, these are *energetic* rather than physical properties. My client and I talked about ponds, both existing and potential. The property already had two ponds and the owners were considering creating a third. The two existing ponds were in a gently sloping meadow in front of the house, an area already energetically female, and my team cautioned not to overdo the water element there by adding more ponds to avoid creating a male/female imbalance. Conversely I was told that adding a small pond on the hillier, more male portion of the land would soften the male energies in that area. I even heard "the sound of water" there, suggesting something already running or flowing, at least energetically, or signaling something that needed to be added.

On yet another property, the owner was planning to build a ceramics studio in one corner of the backyard, and I was told to talk with him in advance of building about the importance of making sure that all four elements were brought into balance on the land. The studio itself would have strong fire (kiln) and earth (clay) elements, and those needed to be counterbalanced appropriately with water and air. Interestingly I saw a "tank of water" in the backyard the first time I worked there, a "pool of water" in the same location a year later; the owner told me he'd envisioned a fountain in that spot so I knew he was already well aligned with water as well as the land overall. He also planned tall ceilings in the studio to assure plenty of air to balance out fire and earth. Although we didn't discuss it, another way of creating the right balance for the air element would have been to work with wind flow on the property.

Stones

Stones are as animate as any other lifeform. They vibrate within a different frequency range than what we've been taught is animate, and they live long relative to humans. Sacred henges and ancient temples around the world, pyramids in the Middle East, Latin America, and Asia, great stone statuary like the moai of Rapa Nui (Easter Island), grand natural formations, and much smaller gemstones, minerals, and crystals all speak to the power and proud heritage of stones.[4]

I came to know stones well while living on Hawai'i Island, where the land is young enough and, in many places, undeveloped enough, that stones abound. The Hawaiians of old built with volcanic stone, and the stony remains of sacred sites and villages long abandoned dot the wooded gulches, fields, and shorelines. Kilauea volcano, on the southeast of the

---

[4] In my work I use the word "stone" to umbrella what a geologist would break down into separate but related categories.

Island and continuously active since its most recent eruption in 1983, keeps giving birth to new land and, as the lava ages and degrades, more and more stones. Old-time Hawaiians say that individual stones can give birth to stone babies, something I have never witnessed nor cannot explain yet do not doubt. Some also say that stones are energetic archives holding the land's stories, and people who know how to listen in just the right way can access those. I have never had that pleasure.

Whatever their composition or configuration, stones can be very communicative land-whispering partners, as my story "The Preferences Of Stones" (pg. 34) makes clear. They may project images, "talk," or radiate strong electromagnetic energy to attract attention to a land issue, especially disrespect. Electromagnetic energy can create persistent problems for anything electronic or battery powered and cause headaches, nausea, and other complaints in humans. On one property I'd been called to, the owner had been mowing over, rather than around, flat stones at the surface of his meadow and there was vigorous gremlin activity on the property to get the owner's attention to change the way he mowed. The gremlins failed at that but they got *my* attention and I mediated the change. Stones who are part of archaeological or sacred sites carry additional energetic layers relating to human intervention, use or abuse, and behavior, and their messages must be heeded if peace and harmony are the goal.

I was surprised at first to learn that stones often are lonely and sad nowadays because few humans understand them as alive and ignore them. In some locales, the grief of stones is palpable. Yet acknowledging their presence with the gentle touch of a hand, a kind word or two, a song or a chant, goes a long way toward mitigating that grief. Like you and me, stones can become depleted or sick, and they can die — something I learned through stone communiqués and experience.

Stones can be good friends and, as I've discovered through land whispering, wise counselors and partners. I must admit I have a soft spot in my heart for stones.

THE PREFERENCES OF STONES

ONE OF MY FIRST CALLS as a land whisperer was to a property whose human stewards wanted to enlarge their small home. This meant moving stones. The couple was aware enough to realize that stones had preferences of their own and asked me to help guide them. A second issue centered on stones that had been bulldozed while the owners were away; it was unclear to me whether the dozer operator had followed the owners' instructions, but in any event the owners were concerned about the status of those stones as well.

As I was new to the practice, I didn't yet have an established way of working so just followed my intuition for the preparatory work before going on site. I sat in meditation at home, connecting with the Stone People and asking for their assistance. They told me that, once on the property, a stone there would attract me and provide further guidance. They also asked me to bring the owl feather on my altar and to weave it into my sweater (not wear it in my hair as an adornment); then they showed me an image of birds flying, which suggested that birds too might be guides on site (which turned out not to be the case, though many birds were present and their presence a delight).

When I arrived at the land, two large stones in the middle of the meadow grabbed my attention and I knew one of them was the guidance stone mentioned during meditation. As my client and I walked around, she showed me what she and her husband were thinking about in terms of remodeling. The home was near the remains of an old stone wall, configured like a "backbone" snaking across the land, and I knew immediately those stones did not want to be moved. The stones told me they had been part of a wall built over 400 years ago (!), though the original wall was no longer intact. They also said they'd be happy to be cleaned of the debris that had settled on or grown over them over time and to be included "as is" structurally as part of an enlarged garden.

The guidance stone then directed me to several piles of large stones elsewhere on the land. My client and I walked around there and talked at several spots where the stones had recently been bulldozed. Not surprisingly, those stones were unhappy about being moved in such a gross, uncaring manner *and* not being consulted beforehand. Yet those same stones were willing to be part of a future garden in that area — an alteration that would require further conversations between humans and stones when the time to plan a garden was right.

This call gave me the chance to talk with people about communicating with stones. The more you connect with one another, the better the long-term relationship will be. You become friends, and trust and respect deepen as they would in any friendship. I told my client how to start talking with and listening to stones, recommending she construct her questions in a yes-or-no format because the answers would be clearer for someone new to subtle-energy communiqués. I also felt that, with her goodwill and awareness, she'd soon be able to glean more than just yes-or-no responses — the stones themselves would bring her along.

I don't know what this couple ultimately decided to do about enlarging their home. But I felt they'd have the proper conversations with whatever lifeforms were involved and abide by the outcomes. ✦

Spirit Nation: the Unseen Ones

I work with a wide array of spirit-beings when land whispering and have come to call the aggregate of this Spirit Nation, or the Unseen Ones.[5] They're "unseen" only in the sense that we don't perceive them with our physical eyes. The Unseen Ones are at the heart of what triggers the call, constitute each interdimensional team, are crucial sources of information, and can hold the key to resolution.

The biosphere, the elements, and stones also are part of Spirit Nation as everything has a spirit, or purely energetic, essence. But they have the additional aspect of manifesting as matter so I've discussed them separately. In a way the distinction is artificial.

Following (in ALL CAPS) are types of Unseen Ones I frequently encounter when land whispering. *Please note*: This listing is *not* exhaustive, and there can be overlap between types. And don't get too literal with the types: this is just a convenient way of categorizing so I can talk about something that is inherently limited by language and cultural mindsets.

As previously noted, GREMLINS are spirit-beings who "misbehave by playing pranks" to get humans' attention about an issue that needs redress. Generally they mean no harm, though there are exceptions. You may recall I had a classic gremlin encounter shortly after moving into a rental house after just coming to Hawai'i (see earlier, "Nature Of The Partnership").

Years later in work for a client, I came upon an unusually active, complex spirit zone, including both playful and aggressive gremlins. In the rambling garage at the rear of the house lived a family of child-like spirits whose gremlin "play" was unintentionally disruptive to my

---

[5] Unseen Ones whose responsibilities are at the planetary level (or beyond) also exist, singly and in councils. I have never knowingly partnered with them as a land whisperer, though I've had contact with and taken instructions from them in my capacity as an Earth worker. "When Land Work Is Earth Work" will give you some idea of what this larger level practice entails.

client. These gremlins were chagrined upon learning they were causing problems and apologized. We agreed that gentle play and limited interaction were acceptable to all, and that resolved that particular issue. But other gremlins in the house caused serious trouble, primarily at night; they pinched, bit, disturbed the humans' sleep, even broke a chair. The reason for their behavior was never clear and they weren't receptive to making agreements as their more playful counterparts were. As it turned out, there was far more to this piece of land whispering than gremlins.

GUARDIAN SPIRITS are ex-humans (the spirits of those once in human bodies) or other types of beings who choose to remain in a place as caretaker-protectors, sometimes for long periods. They have a love of place, a connection too strong to relinquish, and/or a responsibility conferred upon them by those unknown or unknowable.

One property I land whispered had a complex ownership history, including feuding and legal issues between prior owners and boundary disputes with neighbors. The property had several houses on it, some of which had been moved there from other locations. The property had even once been a junkyard. Overall, the energies of multiple owners, tenants, and provenances were entangled.

One of the houses, about 75 years old, had been inhabited for years by the original owner's grandmother during her lifetime. I sensed the grandmother's energy when walking the property with my client (who, I later learned, knew this spirit-being well!). Then, during the clearing process, I discovered that the grandmother-spirit had remained on site as a guardian to continue taking care of the place much as she'd done during her physical lifetime and to remain close to her family, who still lived nearby. As it turned out, she took my team's presence as an opportunity and asked for assistance with leaving — that is, she was ready to transition to the next level. In fact, her readiness to leave was part of the call.

SPIRITS OF PLACE are the demographically diverse energies belonging to a particular "home base." They share the responsibilities and tasks related to that space, are avid partners with human land whisperers, and are always part of the interdimensional team for a given call.

DARK ENERGIES are the product of, and are themselves, power distortions. As projections of the unconscious, of the unhealed self, they feed on negativity and can grow potent, even malevolent. They can be at the root of persistent conflict or violence, addiction, manipulation, dangerous game-playing, or profound heaviness from a cascade of losses and deep grief. Whenever I encounter or sense I *may* encounter dark energies, I ask my team for extra protection in case there's conscious intent to harm. All that said, I have compassion for dark energies as they are caught up in a web not of their own making.

TRAPPED OR LOST SPIRITS are periodic communicants during land whispering. *Trapped spirits* are those stuck in the Earth plane after their physical bodies have died and unable to transition; they may be trapped singly or en masse for long periods. *Lost spirits* are those unaware of their body's physical death, confused about their situation, and thus unable to transition; they often are the product of sudden, traumatic death such as an airplane crash, a drowning, a shooting, or a terrorist attack. Either way, these spirits need help from a land whisperer and team.

I've only encountered trapped and lost *human* spirits. But other lifeforms may experience these states as well and, like humans, need help transitioning.

MALE AND FEMALE ENERGIES represent the two fundamental, complementary, and (when in balance) harmonious aspects of all life, as beautifully illustrated in the classic Chinese yang/yin icon most of us are familiar with. Everything has a male and female aspect regardless of its gender or lifeform, as these are *energies with associated qualities*. The land too reflects the relationship of male and female energies through-out its diverse population and as a whole, and wherever male or female energy is overbearing or insufficient, a land whisperer can help restore the balance.

UNIVERSAL ENERGIES are arguably the most powerful of the Unseen Ones because their domain is planetary and beyond. They include elementals — fire, water, earth, air — which show up under different names and in different guises in different cultures; archetypes like creator-destroyer deities and cosmic twins; and enlightened ones and redeemers like Jesus the Christ and the Buddha. I will leave it at that here…whole books have been written on members of this demographic layer of Spirit Nation.

A COMMUNICATIONS PROTOCOL

Ready to try communicating with other lifeforms? If so, I offer the follow-ing basic protocol to get you started. If you pursue land whispering as a practice, you'll develop your own individual way of working through experience. This is how my practice evolved.

In the beginning, connecting and communicating with other life-forms may feel, well, weird. But that's only because it's unfamiliar. That feeling will pass as you internalize, then customize, your own approach. After a while, it will feel natural and everything will go in automatic.

I strongly recommend you work *on site*, rather than *remotely*, when you're first learning to communicate. On site, your subtle senses attune to the vibrations of the space while you're physically in it, and your five physical senses add cues and helpful associations. When you're more experienced and confident about the process and your abilities, then start communicating remotely — that is, making a conscious connec-tion with a site when not physically on it and at any physical distance from it. Remember: *energetic pathways are nonlocal, extending globally and beyond*. Access is through *intention*.

Please note: The following protocol is meant to familiarize you *only* with learning how to connect energetically with other lifeforms so you can communicate. This provides the foundation for the more advanced work of partnering with an interdimensional team in a land-whispering session to address issues requiring more than simple communiqués. See "A Land Whisperer At Work" for the full range of issues and processes as well as a sample session.

- *Set intention and consciously connect.* Quiet your mind and body, as you would to meditate, and express your intention (silently or aloud) to communicate with a particular land complex. If there's any uncertainty about where you mean, name or describe it. Then ask (silently or aloud) to be connected to the spirits of place and allow a few seconds for the connection to stabilize. Whether you can sense the connection or not, trust that it has been made.

- *Be courteous and greet the space.* If you're new to the land, introduce yourself (silently or aloud) as you would to anyone you meet for the first time, especially a potential partner. If this is your home and you're already well acquainted, say hello as you would to a good friend. You can be more elaborate or ritualistic, but that's a matter of personal style, not necessity. Greeting the land may feel strange at first. Later on it will feel strange *not* to offer a greeting. Throughout your interaction, continue to observe social courtesies as you would with a human friend or partner.

- *State your reason for communicating.* Be complete and specific, don't make assumptions, and be conscious of the language you use, as spirits tend to take things literally much as human children do. Be humble and appreciative. If you have a request, make it. But be careful what you ask for: you might get it *and* it may not manifest in the form you expect it to or hope for!

- *"Listen" with all your senses for the land's response.* The land *will* respond, but you must be open to perceiving that response however it's delivered: an image or sign; a word, phrase, or conversation (some spirits are very chatty); a feeling; or some combination. Remember: the subtle world can be *very* subtle (recall "Tips for working with subtle energy"). Know that the entire entourage — all lifeforms on macro and micro levels across multiple dimensions — is taking your measure. Also know that, over the longer term, and especially if this is your home space, as trust grows the land will reveal more and more to you whenever you connect.

Remember too that the land has its own needs and preferences, which may not fully align with yours. If you have a request, you may need to keep communicating till an understanding has been reached and you're clear about proceeding. An aware steward (and sensitive partner) is willing to be inconvenienced, compromise, and reformulate plans.

- *Consciously disconnect with thanks.* When your communications feel complete, ask to be gently disconnected from the land complex and close by *expressing your gratitude*. Remember, this is a *partnership*.

A Land Whisperer At Work

"There are no sacred and unsacred places, there are only sacred and desecrated places... The answers [to how to put the big things right] will not come from walking up to your farm and saying this is what I want and this is what I expect from you. You walk up and say what do you need..."

— Wendell Berry, in an interview with Bill Moyers on
Moyers & Company, October 6, 2013

"That country knows who is walking about in it. It can feel who is there..."

— an Australian Aboriginal quoted in *The Way of the Earth*,
T.C. McLuhan, 1994, Simon & Schuster, NY

Getting To Know The Land

Once you've begun connecting energetically with some of your relations and have enough of a communications process in place, you're ready to take the next step: *creating a relationship or, more precisely, a set of interlinked relationships*, with an environment and, over time, with multiple environments.

Getting to know the land is much like getting to know people. How you connect with all those in a given land complex depends on your abilities, your inclination, and the specific situation. In Hawai'i, where I came to my calling as a land whisperer, my relationships with the land I lived on and with for 16 years were ongoing and deepened over time as they would in any healthy long-term partnership. In contrast, where I'm called to serve someone else's land, the situation is tailored and the period of involvement brief unless the place is one I return to for repeat work.

Land work & the country

When I'm land whispering in rural areas, my principal relationships are with the *natural environment* — biological lifeforms, the elements, stones — and the *spirits of place*. I'm also in relationship with the *human-built environment*, and though there's less of it than in more developed areas, it's still significant. For instance, an old farmhouse or shed may hold energetic issues of consequence to the larger story.

If I'm new to the land, I take the time to walk it solo or with my client, depending on the situation, to start getting the feel of the place and connect energetically. If it's acreage, I walk as much as I'm physically capable of and time and the terrain allow. If the land in question is very large (many square miles), like forest, rangeland, or a park, I walk only a small portion and connect with the whole energetically, sending my greetings out over the airwaves and staying tuned for the response. If the land is too far away for me to be physically present

— it might be across the country or, for that matter, half way around the world — I proceed strictly energetically, doing the entirety of the work remotely.

Land work & the city

When I'm land whispering in a more developed area, my principal relationships are with the *human-built environment* — residences, commercial centers, public spaces — simply because there's so much of it and, as always, the *spirits of place*. The spirits are just as present and active in the built environment as they are elsewhere. In fact, urban spirits may have a lot to communicate to a land whisperer because of all the human impact there. I'm also in relationship with the *natural environment*, but less directly because so much else has been superimposed upon it.

Remember: the human-built environment is animate. As previously noted in "All Our Relations," constructions are crafted from Earth-sourced materials, manufactured using natural elements and forces, and infused with their designers' and builders' energy. An entire city, a neighborhood, an urban park, a marina, a theatre, a bridge, a skyscraper, a subway system, a mall — all are inspirited.

As in the country, I walk the area to the degree possible and connect energetically on site and/or remotely.

Structures & interiors

I work extensively with interiors because people live and conduct much of their business within structures. Entering into relationship with a home or workplace, or with large, heavily trafficked public spaces like airports, malls, and civic centers, is as important as getting to know the ground they stand upon. It may be even *more* important because we humans now spend so much time indoors. In fact, my body is an especially strong barometer indoors because the structure acts as a physical container concentrating and even amplifying the energy there.

Interiors may feel uncomfortable in whole or in part. I often perceive areas of dense energy indoors — that is, areas where old, stagnant energy has concentrated over time. I sense this as pressure at my temples and queasiness in my stomach, a strong sign that the interior needs to be cleared. Another land whisperer might sense it differently yet come to the same conclusion.

Because interiors are defined containers, they're also great places to learn about how spatial arrangements affect energy flows. This is key not only to good health but also to productivity and prosperity, as anyone familiar with feng shui knows. Land whispering and feng shui are related practices and may complement one another neatly. But, to the best of my knowledge, land whispering goes deeper than feng shui through clearing, scouring away the old patterns that might otherwise undermine feng shui placement.[6]

THE CALL

The land holds imbalances until Nature deems it just the right time for just the right person to be tapped to help restore harmony. The trigger for this restorative work is known as the *call*. The call is one more indication of how vital the land-human partnership is, and of how interdependent we humans and all our relations are.

The call may be gross (easily perceived) or subtle. It may be direct (an energetic message to you from the land itself) or indirect (an energetic message framed as a "problem" and brought to you by a potential client). And because energy isn't constrained by physical space, the call may come from halfway around the world, the work to be done

---

[6] My reference to feng shui is to current practice. It's possible, even likely, that feng shui was practiced differently in ancient times than it is today, and there may have been clearing protocols.

remotely. Through practice and experience, you'll become more and more attuned to "hearing the call" and distinguishing it from your own thoughts, desires, and agendas, which are *not* appropriate bases for land whispering.

If you're uncertain about the call, sit quietly and ask Nature for verification or more information and don't go forward unless you're clear. Trust that whatever information you do receive is all you need to proceed. Remain centered within your intuition and keep your intellect out of it for now.

THE TEAM

No human does land whispering solo! It takes a team: a land whisperer in collaboration with an *interdimensional team,* or *i-team* for short. Think of the i-team as a uniquely configured council convened to serve the highest good of a particular place. Because i-teams are drawn from a demographically diverse spirit population, the more adept you are at communicating energetically — that is, at whispering — the better.

My role as a land whisperer is something like that of an orchestra conductor or committee chairperson: I invite an i-team into session once I'm called and ready to work, and I oversee the process till completion. Every team member plays a unique part and has unique responsibilities; no one is more or less important than another, including me.

I have a set i-team protocol for clearings (see "A Sample Clearing Session"); some team members are a core group who participates every time, and others are site or situation specific. Other types of land work may require a different team configuration. Although inquiring minds may want to know who's on the team, it's unlikely you'll be able to identify every single member — and that doesn't matter because, when everything's aligned, the perfect team shows up. Trust Nature!

Assessing The Situation

Like any healer, a land whisperer both *diagnoses* and *treats*. Assessment is the *diagnostic process of sensing the condition of the land complex on a given site once you've been called*. With your i-team's help, you discern issues and patterns that need to be redressed through clearing or other actions. Assessment may be done on the physical site, remotely, or (my process) via some combination of the two.

Every land whisperer has a unique way of assessing the situation, and what follows here are key points from mine as it has evolved over time. Once again, I offer my approach as a model, a starting point, for your own.

Before going to a site, I prepare by checking in remotely for initial impressions and guidance; this is quick, less than 10 minutes. This is not the time to investigate, just to receive a few key, orienting hits. I sit quietly, intentionally connect to the space in question, ask for whatever information is available and appropriate, and remain open to receive whatever comes in whatever form (image, voice message, impression, emotion, bodily sensation).

I'm protected energetically as soon as I respond to the call. It's automatic. But I may ask for extra protection if a situation feels uncomfortable or potentially harmful. Not all beings are benign and it's as important to take appropriate precautions in land whispering as it is in a physically hazardous situation.

When on site with a human client, we do a walk-through. I listen carefully to what the client says spontaneously and to the answers to my questions, some prompted by being there or our conversation and some by my pre-site prep. I also get a direct "first feel" of the space. Where a site is so large it cannot be walked in its entirety, I may ask additional questions. If it's not possible to go on site, I communicate with my client by phone, email, or skype and occasionally request a photo or two (helpful but not required); the rest is done remotely. The reality is: I can do *everything* remotely, but on-site impressions and personal interactions add information and satisfy our human need for contact.

When the land is the client — that is, when the land calls directly, with no person as intermediary — the process is the same except of course for the human interaction.

My first calls as a land whisperer were nearby, and after prepping I'd go to the site and both diagnose and treat there with my human clients. After serving several clients, I changed my way of working after pre-site prep: I now do a first phase of the assessment on site whenever possible but everything else — the rest of the assessment and the treatment — in a remote session at home. Doing the whole process on site made the work seem too much like a performance, and I felt constrained to interact fully with my i-team.

You can do remote work anywhere but it's best to have a dedicated space you use consistently. The work consecrates the space, and you can manage the energy there, assuring all is clear and well protected.

Assessment proceeds a little differently each time. Some assessments take longer than others irrespective of the acreage or complexity of the call, and some yield far more conscious information than others. I've learned to trust that I'll receive whatever's needed — no more, no less — to move from diagnosis to treatment.

ISSUES & PATTERNS

The call to land whispering arises from a situation requiring redress. But the issue triggering the call may turn out to be a nominal or *surface* issue — that is, a symptom — rather than the *source* issue — that is, the root cause. A surface issue may just be the "hook," something provocative and attention-getting. The truth is: Nature uses whatever's handy to draw balance to the space.

SOURCE ISSUES fall into four interlinked categories:

1. *Lack of respect and honoring*, usually due to lack of awareness, including failure to ask permission of the land complex for site alterations or other human-initiated activities.

2. *Loss*, felt by humans, other lifeforms, and the land as a whole, including
   » grief over loss of human contact by other lifeforms in the land complex
   » grief over loss of the old ways of life which naturally include respect and conscious partnering, especially for indigenous peoples, and often expressed by the spirits of place
   » grief over loss of tribal lands, frequently resulting in illness, addiction, and death (the land is a key part of the immune system)
   » loss of identity because place names have been changed or areas radically altered
   » loss of the land as sanctuary, as a place of healing, renewal, and privacy
   » loss of the land as a special place to which a human or community has longstanding connections that then are severed
   » loss of vitality within the land complex where reciprocity within the partnership has been inadequate, as in my story "One Hand Washes The Other" (pg. 54)
   » loss by a human or ex-human of an idea or intention, a dream or desire, related to the land, as in my stories "The Horsewoman And The Ghost Corral" (pg. 56) and "All In The Family" (pg. 58).

3. *Soul work*, including the need for *soul release*, as for trapped, lost, or guardian spirits ready to transition, and *soul retrieval for the land itself*, as for places suffering extreme or repeated trauma because of war, toxic dumping, natural disasters, terrorism, human trafficking, drug houses, and so on.

4. *Recurring patterns of disharmony over long periods*, usually born of persistent conflict, abuse, war, or other violence; this also may involve distortions such as dark energies resulting from unhealed human emotional wounds, as in my story "Déjà Vu All Over Again" (pg. 60), and portals (energetic doorways allowing access to and from other dimensions).

SURFACE ISSUES take many forms, as the following list, by no means exhaustive, reflects. It's important to understand that a surface issue isn't a trivial issue; it is valuable and must be honored and addressed but it doesn't tell the whole story. It's also important to understand that a surface issue in one situation could be a source issue in another situation; discerning this is part of the assessment and depends on context:

» Death due to violence, illness, suicide, or "accidents"

» Illness, especially serious and prolonged illness

» Lack of mental clarity

» Poor productivity of gardens and crops; imbalances in water, soil, minerals, or microbes, leading to pest or other problems

» Rapid turnover of property owners or businesses in the same location

» Unusual, unexplained occurrences involving gremlins and/or other spirit demographics, as in my story "Life At Spirit Central" (pg. 64)

» Poor neighbor relations, including boundary issues, physical and/or energetic violation, and manipulation, as in my story "Horse Sense" (pg. 67)

» Site problems that are part of a larger situation in a neighborhood

» Dense or "heavy" energy; discomfort on site for no apparent reason

» Imbalance of male/female energies on a site

» Complex site histories, especially where structures have been moved from one site to another, causing energetic entanglement

» Serious substance abuse; drug houses

» Legal problems, including court cases, incarceration, fraud/embezzlement, nonpayment of or default on moneys owed, property issues

» Recurrent disharmonious patterns of behavior, site usage, interpersonal dynamics, and so on, sometimes for long periods

Issues can create patterns because, in the world of energy, "like attracts like." A particular issue will draw to the space more of the same issue — that is, more of what caused the imbalance in the first place — and, given enough time, those recurrences form a pattern. This dynamic creates a positive feedback loop: the greater the number of situations sourcing from a particular issue, the more entrenched the pattern, and the more entrenched the pattern, the more such issue-based situations will arise. What shifts this feedback loop is *clearing,* my major task as a land whisperer. *Clearing old energy patterns breaks the cycle.*

ONE HAND WASHES THE OTHER

I WAS ASKED INFORMALLY by an acquaintance to assess the condition of his land while we both participated in a workshop there. I believe the owner sensed something was wrong, which was why he asked, though I don't know whether he ever acted on my information.

The property, about 3 acres, had a home and several other structures on it at the time, with more planned. It also had an amphitheatre and grass "stage" where a segment of the community gathered periodically for dance, music, and other artistic or playful events.

The land felt neglected and depleted. Some areas were cluttered with debris, diminishing the natural beauty and contributing to energetic stagnation; the large meadow was overgrown; and the stones I touched felt "tired," something I'd never experienced before. The male-female energies were out of balance (too much male, not enough female). A friend of the owner's lived on site and had caretaking responsibilities, though it seemed to me he wasn't doing enough, and his intense male energy exacerbated the existing male-female imbalance. This land needed real gardeners, knowledgeable and dedicated, not occasional helpers or those with a more superficial, even if sincere, understanding of how to tend things.

People came and went on the property for various reasons and durations, leaving in their wake energetic entanglements. The owner himself traveled quite a bit and I sensed the land often felt abandoned by him. The spirits of place knew his original intention, to create a model for sustainable living, yet something else, something less noble, was playing out.

The community gatherings at the amphitheatre, intended to "feed the space" from a perpetual "energy pool," were instead draining it, the attendees taking too much and not giving enough back. The land needed to be replenished consistently and lovingly to be able to continue giving at this level. Reminiscent of the M.C. Escher lithograph *Drawing Hands*, in which each hand draws the other with infinite reciprocity, one hand must "wash" the other if the land is to maintain a healthy state or, in this case, be restored to health. As things stood, the "pool" was near to bone dry.

The day after the workshop in a morning meditation at home, I was instructed to send loving energy to this land. I had asked the workshop participants to do this with me the day before, but it was late in the program and their energy, individually and as a group, was patchy and their focus wandered. They were only "day-trippers" after all, with no real connection or commitment to the place.

Nevertheless for me this was a call. I had to respond. I *wanted* to respond. So my team and I enfolded the land in a golden bubble to begin re-energizing it. Much more was needed on an ongoing basis, but that was the landowner's responsibility. Ultimately it always is. ✦

THE HORSEWOMAN AND THE GHOST CORRAL

I WAS CALLED TO CLEAR A PROPERTY the owner was intending to put on the market. He had built — indeed was still completing — a large custom home with a unique geometric design. The higher elevation location was dramatic and the land powerful, with a strong Hawaiian cultural vibe. It's unusual for someone to invest a great deal of love, thought, care, time, and money into building a home for himself and then immediately plan to sell, but unexpected circumstances had dictated the decision.

Construction had taken far longer than anticipated, involving four different contractors, two of whom turned out to be unethical, accepting money and then skipping out before completing their work. Even more significant, the home had been conceived and begun to be built when the owner's girlfriend at the time developed cancer and subsequently died. She was on property when ill and dying; a memorial service was held there after she passed and her ashes scattered on the land. Her energetic presence remained strong, as if her spirit had unfinished business, and was negatively affecting the owner's current relationship.

Every call to land work has an underlying issue or pattern as well as a related central focus. In this case, the pattern was loss: multiple issues of loss needed to be addressed and cleared so the property would be "free" to sell and everyone, including the girlfriend's spirit, could move on. The focus was indeed the girlfriend who'd died, but not entirely in the way I'd imagined — which is why it's so important to learn to distinguish thoughts (mental constructs) from intuitions and higher guidance.

The girlfriend's spirit and I connected easily and communicated well. Perhaps she was relieved to have someone she could finally talk to! I saw how deeply she was mourning and assumed (wrongly — don't assume!) this had to do with her lost future with the owner. She was a horsewoman, and the area directly in front and down slope of the house had been intended as a large corral and riding arena. I had sensed "ghost horses" at the end of my on-site assessment but didn't know what to make of that at the time.

What I learned through our communication was that her pain was about the *horses* or, more precisely, the *dream* of the horses and plans for the arena! She'd continued holding onto all this as if she were alive and the plans could be made manifest. She did this even knowing she was dead (I asked); some spirits don't realize their human container has passed and need help acknowledging it so they can transition. This part of the session was emotionally charged. Land whispering may seem abstract in the telling but it is not so in the doing! Finally, my i-team gave the horsewoman-spirit the permission she needed to let go of the dream. She expressed gratitude and relief. We all understood then that *everyone* was now free.

Several days after clearing had completed, the owner emailed with an awe-filled confirmation of the success of the work. Just one night short of full moon, from his lanai he saw an intense rainbow that had formed over the arena area — and *only* this area was illuminated by moonlight. He could make out several bands of color within the rainbow. Several rainbows had formed over the property during the day as well. We see lots of rainbows in Hawai'i, but some rainbows and rainbow-laden situations are far more unusual than others, and this was one of them. The owner found it all (his word) "incredible!"

I learned months later that the owner and his current girlfriend had married — and were living in the home he'd planned to sell but didn't have to thanks to the gifts of the spirits and the magic of land whispering. ⬅

All in the Family

A REALTOR CONTACTED ME ABOUT A LISTING, now hers, for a property that had been in and out of escrow for four years. She knew something was wrong and felt I'd be able to discern what and help resolve it.

The owner of the 7-acre parcel, which included a house and decrepit barn, had died 8 years earlier. The house was in far better shape than the barn but did need work; it didn't feel as bad energetically as I thought it might. The crawl space was jam-packed with old tires, other auto parts, marine equipment, and much more — a chaotic dumpsite that ran the length of the house and needed to be cleared physically and energetically.

The realtor and I both felt the owner's spirit, whom we came to call Grandpa, as we walked the site. The property had been a family compound during the owner's lifetime; the place was special to him because of that, and his spirit clearly retained those feelings, or their imprints, in whatever way spirits do. In fact, the owner had wanted one of his granddaughters to live there after his passing, but they resided far away and no one was up for a move. Some family members stayed temporarily after his death and cleared out the barn, but then left. Grandpa was very unhappy about his reluctant heirs and expressed his displeasure by souring prospective sales. I knew the bulk of my work would center on a serious conversation with Grandpa and hoped I could find the key to helping him let go.

Opening the remote session at home, I invited Grandpa in with my team. I began by inquiring how we might help, and he responded, "Nobody ever asked me that before!" He was very emotional and remained so throughout the rest of the session.

We talked about family — the heart of the matter — and in that moment I was guided to the key: that *family goes beyond blood.*

"If we called in someone from your *spirit* family, your *extended* family, as the next steward," I said, "would that be acceptable?"

Grandpa said he'd never thought of that before and liked the notion very much. So as a group, we sent out that request.

I reminded Grandpa that, in continuing to show the property, realtors would bring people to the land who were not "part of the family," but told him not to worry, the right one would show up. I also explained the clearing process I was about to set up, figuring it was unfamiliar and might cause anxiety, even fear; I didn't want to lose his trust and assured him clearing would benefit his goal.

We also discussed the idea of a brief guardianship once the new steward came onto the land — that is, Grandpa would serve as a temporary overseer-assistant until the newbie had settled in. I felt this would help everyone with the ownership transition. But I made clear that *guardianship* wasn't *control*.

"You have to trust and let go," I told Grandpa.

I also told him he was free to transition at any time and we'd help — all he had to do was ask. I thought he might be ready once the new family member took over stewardship, as there'd no longer be any need for him to stand guard.

As clearing activated, I saw a golden bubble around the house and blue energy inside, where little spirits were dancing in a circle. I became aware of one other guardian on site, but evidently that being and Grandpa had a good relationship, perhaps even an agreement, as no issues arose. All seemed in alignment...

Several weeks later, the realtor emailed me to say one of the former prospective buyers warned off by Grandpa before land work had resurfaced and made another offer, and the property was in escrow. I had to smile at that. I hoped Grandpa was smiling too. ⬸

DÉJÀ VU ALL OVER AGAIN

AT TIMES, THE IMBALANCES I'M CALLED TO WORK WITH are less about a particular land complex and more about the current steward's unhealed wounds, which are carried along when that person moves from one property to another. There may even be the tendency to sell and buy more frequently or go from rental to rental in an unconscious attempt to leave the trouble behind. But that doesn't work. Instead, the same basic story repeats itself at each new place until — ideally — the steward is aware enough and willing to address the source issue. We humans are as much a part of the land complex as any other lifeform and may ourselves be the nexus of what begs for resolution.

An acquaintance asked me to do a remote clearing on property she owned in another state. She had resided there for a long period and raised her children there, but the time had come for her to sell. She called the place "haunted," "troubled," and also referred to "dark energy"[7] on site, though it wasn't clear to me then what she meant by that.

She had bought the place from a man who had emphysema and was alcoholic. There were two rundown structures on the land: a funky house and a shack. She renovated both, enlarging and beautifying the house over the years and turning the shack into a lovely rental cottage. Later on, when in the process of retiring, she moved into the cottage and rented out the big house. That's when things began to go awry. The new renter was difficult to get along with, possibly manic depressive. Upon learning the property was about to go on the market, she became vindictive, damaging the house badly and calling in the county about some of the renovations,

---

[7] See "Spirit Nation: the Unseen Ones" in the main text and the Glossary for more about dark energy.

which, it turns out, were unpermitted. The upshot was a long, legally fraught, and costly process for the owner.

As we talked more about my client's personal history, she told me she'd had cancer and admitted she also had had an alcohol problem, speculating that there might be a pattern of addiction associated with the property. I would add to that, a pattern of illness.

I completed the assessment remotely and my i-team and I did a clearing. I learned more about the dark energy then; it was associated with on-site violence that was hundreds of years old *and* with my client's unhealed self, and both were addressed during the session. My client traveled to the cleared property shortly after land whispering to prepare it for sale and told me the change there was "astounding."

Although we hadn't spoken about it, I was aware of another property my client had owned, this one in our community. I'll call this property #2. I don't recall whether she herself had ever lived there (perhaps at first?), but it too was, or had become, a rental that turned over several times during her ownership. I knew from direct experience that most of those renters brought unsettled, even chaotic energy to the space, and there also were hostile interactions between my client and a neighboring landowner. I pondered the similarities between the two properties. Troubled and troublesome renters…difficult interpersonal dynamics…possibly dark energy… Was this a pattern? With only two properties, it's hard to say. I asked my i-team about investigating #2 further and was told not to: this was not part of the call.

A month later, this same client contacted me about her current residence — property #3 — and as we walked the site and talked, a remarkably familiar story emerged. My client had built two houses on this land, the first her own residence (very small initially and later enlarged), the second a rental. There was yet another toxic renter. Interestingly, she then brought up property #2, again mentioning "dark energy" and describing her first renter there as "toxic." As we continued our discussion, my client spoke more deeply about herself — about how she was at a crossroads in life and needed clear space in which to sort things and make good decisions. I could really feel her woundedness, and saw how that attracted more of the same. But I also knew she was savvy enough to perceive this and wondered whether she was really asking for help or just playing games. Or maybe both?

In session, I was given no additional information about the older patterns on the land, as is often the case. Instead the work focused on *my client's* recurring pattern. I asked for her pattern and the associated woundedness to be cleared, and from its source, whatever that may be.

As I held the space for clearing, a much younger version of my client appeared. The number "18" came to mind and I took that to mean this was her 18-year-old self. I knew intuitively her pattern related to this younger self but was given no details, and I shared this information with her in an email. In reply she told me that around age 18 she'd turned from "good girl" to "bad girl," but kept her "bad" self under wraps, presenting her "good" face to the world. I suspected she was still doing this. She admitted she had work to do on herself! And…although I accepted this as sincere, I also knew the "bad girl" would be reluctant to give up power.

Five months later, this client contacted me yet again. She was in the process of purchasing a condo in a golf-course community to use as a vacation rental. This seemed a strange investment choice to me: the condo's current owners hadn't made much money from renting it and the financial times were dicey. Though this situation differed somewhat from what I'd worked with previously for this client, there were echoes of the old pattern.

A misunderstanding with the lender created mortgage problems, which set the loan process back and amped up the interest rate, and a several-year dispute between developers and local groups was ongoing and its outcome unpredictable. Fierce battles had been fought in the area centuries back, and it was crucial to clear those old imprints and minimize battle energy as an attractor. But what troubled me most was what (again) felt like energetic game-playing, the "bad girl" calling the shots. Playing games with the spirits, especially powerful ones, is foolish, disrespectful, even dangerous. The condo purchase felt risky to me on multiple levels and I told my client so. Nevertheless she chose to go ahead with it and the deal closed a month later.

Several months afterward, my client emailed to say she wished she'd heeded my warnings about the property, rattling off a string of problems since she took ownership: a rock through the bedroom window, major repairs of things that had passed the home inspection, termites, a leak in the roof, changes in management and disclosures of financial mismanagement, and poor bookings. She asked if we should do another clearing.

I told her bluntly that her old pattern was still in force and that until she addressed it — the work for now was *hers* — doing another clearing was pointless. I'm not even sure the i-team would have agreed to assemble. I gave my client guidance on how to proceed. I knew she was totally capable — assuming she wanted to create a shift.

I did no further land whispering for this client and don't know whether "bad girl" surrendered her domain or not. Old patterns are the devil to ferret out, their neural pathways deeply grooved. To effect change, there have to be strong desire and a big enough payoff, and the courage to leave behind what's familiar, no matter how distorted. ◆

LIFE AT SPIRIT CENTRAL

I WAS CALLED TO A RENTAL PROPERTY by a friend on behalf of the young couple living there amidst an unusual level of spirit activity. The initial report included two entities who were "pissed," pinching the residents and disturbing their sleep; something "growling" in the banana patch just outside the house; and a female spirit who vomited, talked quickly, then disappeared. The couple wanted to move but my friend thought the house was, for whatever reason, holding them there.

The couple lived in a small apartment behind a vacant house with a large, rambling garage in back and a productive vegetable garden. Immediately I was made aware of five spirits who might need help, possibly with transitioning; three were trapped and two were there by choice as guardians. Of the three trapped, one was a murder victim from more than a century ago and the other two were related to the person murdered.

My client (the young man from the couple) described a highly active spirit zone, especially at night. He had encountered a "Hawaiian elder" guardian and a "little girl" (seen by a variety of people, as it turns out), as well as a host of others, some resident but many transient, moving through a "pipeline" that bisected the living room. Some spirits were aggressive (pinching, biting, and so on); one broke a chair. Others were benign. Some were humanoid, whereas others manifested as "electric sparks."

The quality of the energy on the property varied. It was dense, heavy, in some places, and generally buzzy (very uncomfortable for me); the densest was in the rambling garage. While talking with my client in the backyard, I suddenly experienced a strange visual distortion, as if I were wearing someone else's glasses. My client was familiar with this phenomenon, remarking that sometimes the "air" appeared colored and "wavy."

The couple was working hard to handle all this, and I hoped my team and I could meet the challenges of this complex case.

I learned more when completing the assessment remotely and activating the clearing. Three of the resident spirits wanted to transition, as did the little girl, who had been looking for her family, and we provided assistance for all four. I saw hands reach out for the little girl — beautiful and touching, as the transition process always is for me. The two guardian spirits were content to remain on site.

I discovered a "family of child-spirits" in the garage, which was not a surprise as I'd sensed something when on site. They had been responsible for the gremlin-like activity, and I negotiated an agreement with them to stop their high-jinx and be respectful of the humans in residence. They hadn't realized they were creating a problem and apologized. We agreed they could be gently playful and occasionally interact with the humans, but nothing more, nothing they now knew to be disruptive. They seemed to understand and were willing to comply.

The "pipeline" was another matter. It felt like a crowded freeway with two-way traffic, spirits moving through with their own agendas and purposes, and some with very different energy. I asked for an agreement on relocating the pipeline so it didn't bisect the living space; further, I asked that the walls of the pipeline be strengthened to minimize bleed-through from other worlds. I saw the pipeline "raised up over the house" — that is, moved to another, less intrusive level.

I asked for protection for the couple to be set after clearing and for all new agreements to be securely in place to assure a more harmonious living environment. A small amount of contact with the guardian spirits and playful gremlins was deemed acceptable to all.

I asked for feedback from my client about a week later as I do when the work is more complex. He told me life had been peaceful initially, but then new activity cropped up at night near the door and bathroom. His wife had heard something running across the roof, the noise consistently in the same spot — she seemed sure it was not a rat or the rattle of banana fronds. Their cat was acting strangely as well, fearful and even hiding.

I investigated further, suspecting a breach in the relocated pipeline. Sure enough, there was a tear and an ex-human had been coming through, seeking a pathway of its own (unsuccessfully). The entity wasn't harmful or rascally, just searching. I asked for help for this spirit, for the tear to be closed, and for the pipeline to be scanned for weak spots and further strengthened.

After additional feedback later on, I told my client that he and his wife would have to move if they wanted a reliably peaceful existence, hoping that my team's work had at least released any energetic hold the house had on the couple. No matter what we did, I felt there would never really be peace at Spirit Central. ✦

Horse Sense

A CLIENT CONTACTED ME for repeat work on her property — a maintenance clearing and an assessment for a new situation regarding infringement by her uphill neighbor. I knew that, whatever else came up, there might be a need for energetic protection after clearing; there often is with boundary issues. This client had three horses, and during my preparation before the site visit, one of them told me that they (the horses) needed help beyond what my client was aware of. The horse did not elaborate, but I knew this would come clear later on.

As my client and I walked the land and talked, I felt strong, uncomfortable, "buzzy" energy directed towards the property from a small house sitting close to one of the uphill neighbor's boundary lines. There were several occupied structures on that property, and a stream of people coming and going. My client and the neighboring landowner, who lived on site, had gotten into several altercations about work going on at the edge of his property, which she felt impinged on her privacy and impacted the fundamental enjoyment of her own land. She also sensed energetic game-playing, felt hooked by it, and wanted help getting "off the hook."

As it turned out, the horses had taken upon themselves the responsibility of warding off or pushing back the "negative" energies pressing in from the neighboring property, especially when my client was traveling and not a physical presence on the land. During her most recent trip, the horses couldn't handle the energies and became quite ill with hoof fungus; by the time she returned, they were seriously hobbled, limping and in pain, and demanded excessive attention before she'd even unpacked her bags. In fact, without realizing it, the horses created a state of emergency that, ironically, added to rather than relieved my client's stress. (A significant point I'll return to later in the story...)

Hoof fungus had been an ongoing problem despite numerous attempts at treatment, and my client intuited that the intense invasive energy had disturbed the soil microbial balance — and *that* was at the root of the persistent hoof fungus. Both the soil and horses needed treatment. This made sense to me, and my team and I would address it in session. As we stood along the pasture fence line and talked over the situation, one of the horses came up to me on the other side of the fence. My client sensed he was the horse who had contacted me during pre-site prep. Then a second horse came over. Both wanted contact and attention, and it was equally clear both were listening to what we humans were discussing.

During the remote session (which also involved issues not mentioned here), I learned more while completing the assessment and before activating the clearing. What had been pushing in from the neighboring property was distorted male energy, which was why it felt so strong, even aggressive, and why neighborly relations had turned into a "pissing contest." And I was again contacted by the horse who had spoken to me during pre-site prep. He explained that the horses were worried about the well-being of my client — this was the help alluded to earlier — and had taken on additional responsibilities in an attempt to relieve her of some. I realized then that, in this case, boundary issues extended beyond physical or energetic boundaries to the limits of appropriate responsibility.

As clearing began, I saw a creamy, opaque, white energy releasing from the ground where the soil microbial imbalance was worst — between the front of my client's house and the uphill neighbor's property. The horses liked to hang out there and I was instructed to tell my client to keep them out of that space till clearing was complete and protection had been set. She did. We learned after the fact there was additional reason for this instruction. Right after energetic clearing, a waterline break flooded that area! Had the horses been there, their hooves would have been mucked up badly, exacerbating the hoof fungus. This is a great example of why it's so important to pay attention to all communiqués when land whispering. Something that seems trivial in the moment or whose rationale is not immediately evident may turn out to be significant later on.

After the whole process completed, I talked with my client about the horses' concerns and how responsibilities might be shared appropriately between human and horses so all parties remained healthy. I suggested she create energetic protocols for assisting the horses while she was traveling, especially since she was away more often now than in years past, and communicate those to the horses before she left so they'd know what to expect. I knew she stayed energetically connected with them, but that alone and the assistance of an on-site caretaker were no longer enough.

For their part, the horses needed to understand not only the limits of their own capabilities but also of my client's. For instance, when she returned from traveling, she needed time to take care of herself — to unpack, shower, eat, rest or sleep, and so on — *before* tending to them. I've learned through study and experience that nonhuman lifeforms don't always understand what humans require to be able to function well. You have to tell them. I felt certain the horses sensed enough and had enough sense to honor these differences now that everyone was on the same page. ✦

CLEARING TO RESTORE BALANCE

Land assessment almost always indicates the need for clearing, *the process in which disharmonious energies and energy patterns, often old and multilayered, are gently released from the land complex and transmuted.* Clearing is fundamental energetic housekeeping, purifying the space and creating a fresh, balanced baseline. Even when there are additional issues to be addressed, it's a rare call that doesn't include clearing.

I do clearing remotely, and directly on the heels of the completed assessment, as I'm already in session with my i-team assembled. I allow about an hour of clock time and work straight through without interruption. I have a pen and notepad handy but keep note-taking to a minimum, as being too mental hampers intuition. Notes are only meant to cue me later on, when I'm documenting the session on the computer and communicating with my client.

Most sites clear within 2-3 days. But some, especially those holding deep-seated energies of conflict, may take longer or may need to be cleared in phases or layers, in more than one session, something you cannot know until you're well into the work.

Both human-caused and Nature-based events can create disharmony that ultimately needs to be cleared. For instance, I was called by both a human client and the land itself to clear the energies of an earthquake in my community in 2006 (see my story "An Earthquake Shakes Things Up," pg. 73). But most land whispering centers on human impacts, and here's why:

When human actions and emotions are unresolved, their energetic imprints become part of the environment in which they were created. This tips the natural balance. If allowed to remain in that environment, the imprints tip the (im)balance even further by attracting other situations with similar imbalances — the energetic dynamic of "like attracts like" (see "Issues & Patterns," earlier in this chapter). The environment falls more and more out of balance until the time is right for a land whisperer to be called to intervene.[8]

We humans have an obligation to help heal the ways in which we've detrimentally impacted the land. This is part of our agreement with Nature, as per the land-human partnership I spoke of early in this book:

> *The land is healed co-creatively.* Nature has agreed to absorb and hold toxic energies resulting from human actions, especially violence, even though this undermines balance for the period such energies are held, and humans have agreed to help transmute those energies — that is, help shift them from one level to another — to restore balance. In this way, the partners share responsibility…

Yet, despite the efficacy of the clearing process, I would be remiss if I did not acknowledge there are instances in which no amount of clearing over any amount of time feels like it can, or will, restore balance. In actuality, in such instances, it may be that given *enough* time, the space will heal. It may be that given *many* clearings over *enough* time, the space will heal. Or it may be that given *many* clearings over *enough* time and with the *right* adjuvant medicine, whatever that may be, the space will heal. In such a situation, "enough time" may mean centuries.

I wrote about one such instance on my website and revisit part of that blog post here to illustrate (www.handonthecavewall.net, *Earth Work Journal*, December 27, 2011):

> *The WTC [World Trade Center] site is, quite simply, a graveyard. Conceived and built for commerce, it became hallowed ground through violent death. There are not only physical remains impossible to identify or recover, but energetic "remains" — souls who have not yet transitioned, the chaotic energies of all thought-forms and feeling-forms from that day [9/11]. Like the toxic dust that has*

---

[8] For more explanation, see *Universal Light Series 2*, Perelandra Center for Nature Research, 1985.

sickened so many, old energies hang around and wreak havoc. And they'll continue to do so long after the rubble has been hauled away, long after a memorial, museum, and new complex of commercial structures have been designed, built, and fully inhabited.

While it's true that energyworkers like me have done healing work there over the past decade [and now, longer], and while it's true that some souls can be assisted and certain energies cleared, and while it's true that the cool, cleansing water of the exquisite memorial — symbolic counterweight to the heat of the attacks — can help heal place as well as people, I believe the WTC space will never be fully harmonized. I believe the energetic imprints from an event of that magnitude will never fully dissipate. I believe this to my core. Put simply, some places — like some people — can never be made whole.

So what does this mean for site renewal?

It means there will be problems. Businesses will fail despite positive projections and solid financing. People will fall ill in unexpected ways. Computer systems will behave idiosyncratically. Lights will come on, go off, at odd hours. Phones will ring in the middle of the night. Anyone sleeping there will have strange and haunting dreams. People who are sensitive will see, hear, smell things that others don't. If you doubt what I posit, just wait and watch...

In rereading my own post, I recognize that words like "never" and "believe" may reveal more about my emotional state when I wrote this than my deeper trust in Nature's transformative power. Still, many places on Earth continue to suffer the energetic fallout of catastrophic events whose full reparations are far beyond the horizon we can see.

An Earthquake Shakes Things Up

A 6.7 MAGNITUDE EARTHQUAKE rattled the island of Hawai'i on October 15, 2006. It was Sunday morning early. I had just gotten up, made myself a cup of tea, and put food down for my cats. Suddenly everything started shaking and I expected that to stop within a few seconds because, in all my years on island, it always had before. A brief shake, a jolt, a wave; a few dishes rattle, the windows flex, then everything quiets. Island residents are used to this: the deep Earth has remained active on the southeast of the island at Kilauea volcano since its most recent eruption in 1983, and a new island, Lo'ihi, now just a seamount, has continued building below the sea's surface some miles offshore.

But not this time. The shaking amped up and up, and everything rocked wildly for 45 seconds. That's a long time when you've lost solid ground. My recollection of that period is fuzzy because I was instantly traumatized; I do remember the contents of cupboards flying out and glass breaking and the house roaring and running around the house screaming, trying to find a safe place when no place felt safe.

A strong aftershock followed minutes later, neighbors checked on neighbors, and cleanup began. Over the next 6 to 8 weeks, lesser aftershocks were frequent and rattled not only our homes once again but our nerves as the Earth took time to find new equilibrium. My cats had bolted from the house when the violent shaking popped off a sliding screen door and ran into the woods. They didn't reappear for days; one wouldn't come to the house and remained terrified for two months. It was hard to sleep for weeks and I felt every little tremor, even the vibration of the wind, in a magnified way.

An earthquake is a release of powerful natural energies — a clearing, if you will — and that clearing has a ripple effect, shaking loose other layers that then need to be addressed. As a land whisperer I knew I'd have work to do.

A call for help came from an acquaintance who'd been through earthquakes elsewhere but had never before had her life turned so upside down. She'd built a tiny house on acreage — her sanctuary! — but lost the feeling of safety and home since the quake and was grieving that loss. Like most of us, she still held earthquake energies in her body — the panic, fright, confusion, and shock as well as the geomorphic vibrations — making her and her three dogs, her dear companions, so uncomfortable she was considering leaving the area.

When on her property, I saw an energetic "cyclone" (vortex) spinning in one corner, sucking deeper Earth energy from the center of the land and creating an "upward drain." A large yellow ring of energy in the center appeared to be a temporary structure meant to help stabilize things and perhaps counterbalance the upward drain. The energy was patchy around the perimeter of the property — in some places comfortable, in others buzzy or causing a queasy sensation. The owner had a sense of vertigo, of things wavering and not being steady or stable. The most heavily impacted area was the dog-agility arena — which was where the owner and her dogs waited out the quake. The dogs had run around wildly and the owner alternately stood and sat (she wasn't stable enough to remain standing). The residue of terror and chaos was palpable.

My i-team and I cleared this acreage of all the earthquake had wrought and whatever was deemed appropriate from older layers (I got no conscious information about the latter and was told I didn't need to know). We also involved the water energies because the water system was precarious and a pond on the property needed attention. The clearing process took nearly 40 hours.

The owner called after the work was complete. She told me she could feel the changes as they'd begun occurring, even before the process had finished, and was excited. The space had been cleared in more ways than one: workers were showing up to do repairs, gardenias were blooming out of season, and — most importantly

— the dogs, even the most sensitive one, were acting much more normal and playful. Companion animal behavior is a telling sign of either balance or imbalance.

When we first met, I'd thought my client's land might need a second clearing but that turned out not to be the case, maybe because I was called directly by the spirits of place of the larger area to do land whispering on "the entire earthquake space" concurrently.

So what exactly was "the entire earthquake space"? Well, that was never made clear, as the quake affected different areas of the island differently and, at 6.7 magnitude, areas up the island chain as well. In cases like this, I trust that whatever's to be addressed will be defined by the Unseen Ones, who know far more than I do. I didn't need to know. I *did* need to execute my instructions: to conduct a clearing, on Hallowe'en, as it turned out, with a larger than usual i-team. The process took 29 hours. Even so, we continued to feel aftershocks, the energies remained disharmonious, and I sensed I'd soon be asked to do further work.

I also had contact with the Earthquake People themselves just after the clearing process, not during it, which would be the norm. In fact, information was slow coming in, and perhaps that was a good thing as we humans can handle just so much at one time and many of us, myself included, were still in shock from the quake experience. Living deep in the Earth, the Earthquake People explained that an earthquake is much like a human migraine — the release of very hot energies upward, layer upon layer rising to the planet's surface and bursting through, shaking things up. The purpose: to shift the status quo.

Concurrently I had a powerful dream about a huge black whale who swam to shore and began eating people. In meditation the following morning, I was told the whales are of the deep Earth and are expressing the discontent of the Deep Ancestors and Earth Keepers about human affairs on the planet. I don't usually think of the Earth as "angry," yet this message of discontent did carry that vibration. It was very strong. Perhaps the quake itself carried that vibration, delivering a message we dared not ignore.

The alert for a second clearing arrived when the dream did, the actual call two weeks later. As my i-team worked, I saw "diagonally striped energy patterns," surprisingly soft green and white, radiating from within the Earth and up through its surface. The second clearing took less clocktime than the first, just shy of 17 hours.

During this period I also was approached by a community member around water issues associated with the earthquake and sensed I'd been called for yet further work. But that's another story… ↚

A Sample Clearing Session

Following is a simple protocol for assessing land and clearing it remotely once you've been called.[9] I recommend using this protocol until you're more experienced and have developed your own way of working. If this is your land and you're physically on site, modify accordingly.

As with previous protocols, the process may feel cumbersome at first, with a lot to remember. But that feeling will pass as you internalize and customize it. After a while, it will go in automatic. In what follows I use language that works for me; yours may be different. As my "Note To Readers" in the front matter of this book makes clear, we simply don't have good language for this kind of practice.

- *Sit in a quiet place where you'll be undisturbed for about an hour.* Allow yourself to settle for a few minutes, become fully present, and slip into a light meditative state. I light a candle to open ritual space. You can skip that or do more, depending on your personal preferences for ceremony.

- *Name the place and assemble your i-team.* Briefly identify the land calling for assistance, and ask the appropriate team to join you. I explicitly invite in the overlighting deva of healing, Nature, the spirits of place (each site has its own), the higher self of every person with responsibility to the land (include yourself), and the Christ energy — that is, the universal regenerative energy of the planet.[10] I may ask for "other beneficent helpers," a catch-all phrase invoking Nature to add to the team other Unseen Ones who are available and appropriate but whom I cannot identify. After concluding the

---

[9] Issues *other than clearing* are not dealt with in this sample session, though the basic process is the same.

[10] This is a reference to *Christ Consciousness*, not to the man Jesus. When in Hawai'i, I came to know this in my work as *The White Light of the Christ Energy as embodied at Mauna Kea*, and once, on the mountain, I experienced it directly — raw, in its pristine state, not transmuted or stepped down — and nearly passed out.

invites, intentionally link energies to form a unified council ready to take action and allow a few seconds for everyone to connect.

- *State your intention for the session.* I talk to my i-team out loud, as if they were people in the room with me, about the call and, as I perceive it, the work at hand. You may prefer to do this silently. Either way, be thoughtful and precise in your language. Take your time and be thorough so you and your team are well aligned.

- *Complete the site assessment if you haven't already.* To recap, I do part of the assessment on the physical site when that's possible and the rest in the remote session with my i-team. This is a real conversation, and I listen to my team as well as talk. Be sure assessment (diagnosis) is complete before moving on to clearing (treatment). I ask my team, "Is that it? Is there anything else I need to know before we proceed?"

- *Set and activate the "clearing container."* I verbally place all issues discerned through assessment "into the container" and ask that the issues and patterns of disharmony be *gently* released (to avoid shocking the land) and transmuted *for the best and highest good of all* (to assure than any agendas, conscious or unconscious, human or nonhuman, are nullified). Nature will protect the historic integrity of the site and ensure that the release includes only what's appropriate in the moment according to the call. I also ask for the space to be *purified* and *set to a new harmonious baseline* after clearing. All this may sound mechanical but I assure you it is not: my demeanor throughout is appreciative, compassionate, and prayerful.

- *Sit quietly and hold the space for clearing.* Once the container is loaded and begins to activate, I sit in meditation for 15-20 minutes (or however long feels rights). I often perceive old energy lifting off the land as a "cloud" that eventually dissipates. You may perceive this differently, or not at all. There is no one right way. Holding the space is a purely energetic process, and running all that energy feels great!

- *Close the session, express your thanks, and stay tuned for check-ins.* Check with your team about when to end the session by simply asking if it's time. I also ask how long the clearing/resetting process will take and when to check back for a status report. Gently disconnect energies with your team members through intention and *thank them for partnering with you.* Remember, this is a collaboration; you cannot do it alone.

  Once the session closes, *the work continues,* overseen by team members tasked with those specific responsibilities (they know who they are — you don't have to). Through periodic check-ins you'll learn when the entire process completes.

- *Document the session.* Details fade quickly from work done in a light meditative state much as they do from the dream state, so I document the session directly after it ends in the work log created on my computer for each case. The log begins when I'm called and ends when the work completes. All entries are dated and comprehensive. If there's repeated work on a particular site, I bring all sessions for that site into one log and sequence them by date.

  The time documentation takes is well worth it, especially as some clients and spaces turn out to be repeat customers. I recommend looking over your work logs from time to time to discern patterns. You also may be surprised at how much you've forgotten, how fascinating the work is, and how you've continued to evolve as a practitioner.

Communications with my human client, if I have one, are an important part of the preceding protocol. After the site visit (or initial conversation if there's no visit), I communicate about when I plan to sit in session, when clearing activates, and when the entire process completes. I share information gained throughout as appropriate — inquiring minds want to know! — using my judgment about how detailed that sharing should be. At times I have specific instructions for clients to help them move forward and *not re-create the patterns that were just cleared.*

Beyond Clearing: Addressing Other Issues

Not all land whispering is clearing. As you become more skilled, and especially if you're called to this practice as a path (see that chapter later on), other types of situations may present themselves, often in conjunction with clearing but sometimes independently.

The stories in this section will give you a feel for addressing issues beyond clearing. Once again, trust that your experiences with the land will deliver whatever training you need and that Spirit Nation will guide you appropriately while you do the work real-time.

Helping souls transition

Souls may end up trapped or lost — that is, unable to transition on their own beyond the Earth plane once their associated physical bodies have died. In my experience, they are likely to require assistance, perhaps because the natural timing of the death-transition process has been disrupted. Helping souls transition is among the most awe-producing work I've ever been privileged to be a part of.

Delayed transitioning can occur for a variety of reasons. Sometimes, souls have agreed to remain on the land as guardians after their physical bodies have died and years later find themselves ready to transition and in need of help then.[11] Other times, especially in the case of sudden and/or violent death, souls may not immediately realize that their physical bodies have died and, when they do later on, are shocked and need to be calmed and reassured before they are receptive to an assisted transition. I've worked with both individual souls and groups of souls in such situations, as the following stories reflect.

---

[11] Site guardians are not necessarily souls of departed humans and could be another spirit demographic entirely.

THE MAN IN A DARK SUIT

A FRIEND AND INTUITIVE HEALER herself contacted me to do a second piece of work on her homesite about a month after my team and I cleared it and put in place energetic protection from an aggressive neighbor. But the new call was of a different order.

Twice, she had perceived an unexplained "figure" when locking up for the night before bedtime. She referred to this figure as "the man in a dark suit." He was in the garage one time, the living room the next. She felt he had presented himself "in a suit" to indicate he was respectable and meant no harm. The spirit world is like that, using what's familiar to us personally and culturally to communicate. This presentation also came across as male. I later was told this was the spirit of an old-time local shopkeeper, which also may explain the suit.

When I checked in energetically, I discerned that the figure was a trapped soul who wanted to transition and "tapped" my client because he knew she would contact me to assist![12] In other words, this was the form the call took. The soul "lived" on a neighboring property, where it had resided with its associated physical body over a hundred years ago. Evidently the person died in his sleep and the soul ended up confused about its circumstances. At first it hadn't realized the associated body had died. Eventually it gained that awareness but didn't know how to transition after so long on its own. My friend and I both sensed the soul was quite lonely.

My i-team and I linked up with this being. As I watched, some team members began escorting the soul along an etheric pathway; he was fearful at first, looking back wide-eyed at the Earth plane, but we did our best to be comforting and reassuring. He soon perceived the souls of those left behind long ago — an emotional reunion for all. The soul grew radiant, crossed some kind of threshold with its brethren…and was gone. ✦

---

[12] Spirits know instinctively who among the living humans on site or nearby are sensitive and will perceive them, making it more likely they'll get the assistance they're seeking.

Warrior Spirits Take Flight

This was my first "official" call as a land whisperer. The experience illustrates what can happen when the call involves a large group of trapped souls ready to transition; the spirit world has quite a communications network, and when there's need, the word goes out. This also was my introduction to energetic pipelines.

ONE MORNING IN 2005, David and I got to talking about his dog walking routes as we sat having breakfast on our lanai in Hawai'i. His least favorite, it turned out, wound through a nearby coastal gulch where, so the stories go, the ancient Hawaiian martial art of lua had been practiced. Lua was used in combat and could be violent in the extreme. David said the imprints of violence in that gulch brought up violent fantasies within him! This took me aback. I realized immediately, instinctively, that those old energies needed to be cleared.

This gulch also is the site of an ancient heiau (temple). Or what remains of it. Though the physical structure no longer stands, the large old stones scattered about the land, its powerful energies are intact. I found them uncomfortable to be around, causing pressure in my head and queasiness in my stomach. I realized I too would benefit from this clearing. Little did I know at the outset just how many beings were to benefit.

I checked in with my guidance about timing and was told not to do anything till the following day, when all would be in alignment for the work.

You don't do land whispering unless it's time.

You don't get called until it's time.

I sat in meditation at home and tuned in the next morning. The energy was heavy, causing pressure in my head just as had occurred on site.

My understanding is that lua had come to be practiced in an unbalanced way. Originally, lua warriors had been taught to both take life and heal it — two radically different intentions — but over time the emphasis had shifted heavily toward killing, and the area I was called to was dense with warlike and "bloody" thought-forms as well as energetic imprints of the blood shed by warriors including those who'd been conquered and sacrificed. In meditation, I perceived spirits that appeared "stuck half in/half out of the ground" and others crying out in despair and agony for release; all were held in the space as if frozen, unable to break free and pass on.

It quickly became evident this was a two-phase healing: (1) violet light would activate and lift off the heaviest (bloodiest, most gruesome) energies; then (2) a golden "blanket" would be placed upon the land to release and transmute whatever remained and purify the space. To conduct the work, I convened a "spirit council" through a battle energy protocol[13] and kept that council in session till the work was complete. I now call that council an i-team.

I also was told that the serene energy of the banyan trees growing nearby helped rebalance land toxic with violence. In fact people tend to plant banyans in such places unconsciously. By asking the banyans themselves, I learned further that they thrive on toxic energy — it's well-matched "fuel"; their many adventitious roots siphon toxicity from the ground into the wood, essentially neutralizing it and holding it for eventual release and transmutation.

I checked in on the clearing process from time to time. Mid-afternoon, a light violet "cloud" of energy sat over a small portion of the area, close to but not penetrating the ground and subtly spiraling or circling. Early the following morning, just a sliver of violet remained, and by midday, a large "bowl" of concentrated brilliant white light had supplanted the violet.

But what I saw then amazed me. Many formerly trapped spirits were "flying out of the land" and up through the white bowl and beyond! It seemed as if there were a spirit pipeline, as if far more

---

[13] From *Universal Light Series 2*, Perelandra Center for Nature Research, 1985; when more experienced, I customized this protocol.

beings than could have been held in that one area alone were streaming out. A pipeline wasn't a stretch at all: Hawaiian heiau are said to be networked energetically, and stones are known to be as well. I asked then that the pace of release be slowed so that proper assistance could be rendered to those being freed. The sudden shift from a long period of entrapment to freedom might be confusing, even traumatizing, to those experiencing it.

The following morning, the land whispering moved into phase two: the gulch was lit with the golden "blanket." Three days later at midday, some golden energy remained in dense, cloudlike patches. Red and white energy joined the gold — the red associated with Pele, the white with Poliahu[14] — and all were set to work together for 48 hours. At my final check-in, I saw the remains of the gold, red, and white, the land "glistening" as if bejeweled.

Healing was complete.

When David again walked this area, he told me the land felt good. The violent fantasies had vanished. He returned several more times over the next few weeks and the clean, clear feeling held. I was eager to walk there as well, to check out the shift for myself. ✦

---

[14] See Great Sisters in the Glossary. Although some of the old stories talk of Pele and Poliahu as competitors and jealous rivals, my experience has been that they often join forces to work for the highest good.

At the Twin Towers

SEVERAL MONTHS BEFORE THE FIFTH ANNIVERSARY of the terrorist attacks on 9/11, I was called to the space of the World Trade Center in NYC. The larger energies leading up to this particular anniversary had been really heavy, almost like a physical weight.

Despite the call, I had to explicitly ask for permission before I was shown any images, a kind of energetic security check. I don't recall ever having to do that before. Once in, I perceived two red-purple "onion-like domes" or "flames," which I inferred to be the energetic remains of the physical Twin Towers. I got so elevated I couldn't verbalize any protocols or talk to my team like I usually do — everything went in automatic and there was little to journal afterward because of my altered state. It's like that sometimes — and a good reminder that you're just one human team member and much larger forces are in charge.

I was told that a clearing had been activated and would take 10 hours, and that lost souls would transition as part of the process

Checking in the following morning, I learned the space was undergoing "blessing" for another 14 hours. I saw subtly dome-shaped golden energy rising between the "Towers." The surrounding energy field was dark, midnight blue, and quite subtle. The whole process was moving slowly — not a surprise considering the dimensions of the original event and the complexity of the space. I perceived the energetic Twin Towers as a gateway, a powerful node in the Earth's energetic grid, each tower a polarity and the golden energy between them a force unifying the polarities.

I did not then, nor later, try to analyze or interpret the images I'm describing here. In revisiting my original journaling, I am grateful I was elevated enough to perceive this information but not so elevated as to be unable to write it down.

The next day, in deep meditation, I saw that the golden, dome-shaped energy rising between the "Towers" had morphed into a double helix spiraling from Earth to the heavens. This flow contained *many souls releasing, transitioning, many more than from 9/11 alone* — that is, souls from older layers as well. I recognized this as a pipeline dynamic, as in my story "Warrior Spirits Take Flight." I also saw, for the first time, that New York City itself is an energetic gateway and that within the bedrock beneath Manhattan is a huge crystalline "world." That "world" looked like a ball of yarn; I could see the "wound threads." Though the winding was chaotic (not what my intellect would expect), nothing seemed amiss.

Overall the energies felt lighter, more activated, than when I was first called to do this work.

Three days after the fifth anniversary of the attacks, I was taken unexpectedly to the World Trade Center site in morning meditation. I'd had no conscious intention of going there, though (with hindsight) the call may have begun the night before when I'd had trouble falling asleep for no obvious reason.

The call was for further soul release. I was given no details about the work, just held the space and allowed those in charge to carry on, trusting as I always do that the right team was there offering the right assistance at the right moment. ✦

Conducting soul retrieval for the land

I was familiar with soul retrieval for individual humans, a practice in which the healer in partnership with spirit allies helps retrieve soul pieces lost due to trauma to facilitate a client's return to wholeness. But it had never occurred to me that land could suffer soul loss as well and require intervention until some years after I'd begun land whispering — that is, until I was called to this particular work for the first time, as the following story recounts.

When living in Hawai'i, I was signaled to check in energetically with the area between the great mountains Mauna Kea and Mauna Loa — "the Saddle" — a powerful landscape where a large army installation also is located. Stories abound about the Saddle; most are historical and cultural, but some recount landings of alien craft and other fringe phenomena. At the time I was signaled, there were concerns among certain community members about a possible increase in military activities to field-test new equipment, and this served as the call. The energies of the Great Sisters Poliahu (associated with Mauna Kea) and Pele (associated with Mauna Loa/Kilauea) made themselves known to me and were ready to collaborate with me and my team, as they'd done a number of times before.

But I found a qualitatively different situation than what I *thought* was the call. This is not uncommon: there's a deeper issue at play than the nominal one, an issue that doesn't show itself until you step in energetically and, even then, sometimes not right away (recall earlier, "Issues & Patterns").

In this case, the land was in shock — numb — a dead zone. Many of the spirits of place had fled. Even though I didn't understand until later why the place was in such a state, I knew the land itself needed a soul retrieval. As I had no established protocol for this kind of work, my team took point and I followed their lead. The team immediately started running energy: gold, to purify; blue to calm. A subtle rainbow of energies soon blanketed the area. I simply held the space and let the interdimensional process work. By the end of this session, I perceived small rainbow "vortexes" (energy spirals), which suggested that some spirits who had fled had begun to repopulate and re-animate the area. Soul retrieval was under way and would complete according to its own timetable. My part was done. Or so I thought…

About two weeks later, my team and I were again called to the Saddle, this time to clear it of battle energy, the *source* issue, as a follow-up to soul retrieval. Our work in this second phase was to help transmute toxic energies within the land from historic battles as well as from more current military activities we civilians can only guess at. The battle energy there must have been fierce to create such a dead zone, and my team and I did everything we could to facilitate healing. Along with my usual protocols for clearing, I used a unique energetic crystal gifted to me some years earlier to connect with the deep Earth and mediate transmutation.

As my practice continues to evolve, I hope to be called more often to do soul retrieval for the land. Considering how much of our planet has been traumatized by conflict over the centuries, I have no doubt there is dire need.

Working with portals

A portal is an interdimensional opening, or "doorway." In and of itself, it's not harmful, but some of what travels between the dimensions linked by a given portal may be. Any portal encountered needs to be carefully assessed, as a couple of examples from my work logs illustrate:

- A portal in the master bedroom of a home with many energetic issues turned out to be an access point to the LowerWorld. While I was sitting in remote session for this site, a friendly, curious being who resembled one of Snow White's Seven Dwarfs (really!) popped out of the portal. It became clear that he and his brethren were simply investigating the home; they weren't behaving badly, they weren't introducing anything harmful nor were they likely to, and they weren't taking anything beneficial away. Nevertheless, after checking I asked that the portal be sealed and locked. As the old saying goes, an ounce of prevention is worth a pound of cure.

■ Two portals in a home posed two very different situations: one (in the backyard) seemed quite harmless, whereas the other (within a family member's energy field) was channeling dark energies sourcing from complex and disturbing circumstances. My team and I worked to close both portals.

Since not all energies in the Universe are benign, as a general rule it's best to seal portals closed *unless* you're instructed otherwise, as in my story "The World Below The Bedroom," or you've been told the particular portal serves a higher purpose and access is well guarded.

THE WORLD BELOW THE BEDROOM

A CLIENT CONTACTED ME about a series of issues on her 3-acre property. The hillside grounds were beautifully cultivated and well maintained. The house was large and multistoried, with spectacular views; it felt like an aerie inside, to the point of being ungrounding. The house interior was, in strong contrast to the grounds, chaotic.

I spent two hours on the property, which is long for an on-site assessment, but this client had so much to tell me I could have been there even longer. The issues included, among other things, violation by neighbors; marital complexities and health problems; intense, old battle energy; strongly aggressive male energy out of balance with the female; and strange stories about the original owner.

There also was "something in the land" causing a problem under the master bedroom. The discomfort was great enough that my client no longer slept in that bedroom; in fact, she was trying out other places in the house to sleep nights and couldn't seem to find the right one. While finishing the assessment remotely at home, I learned that the south end of the house, where the master bedroom was situated, was built over a powerful natural rock formation. I concluded that what my client was experiencing was a lot of raw power from that formation, something I hoped to mitigate especially once the male/female energies were rebalanced.

My team and I did a clearing and worked as appropriate with the other issues, including putting protection in place to counter violation. Client feedback made clear the need for a second remote session — there had been improvement, but with this much going on, with this many layers in the mix, the necessity for further work was not a surprise. Second sessions are rare for me, but they do occur.

What *was* a surprise was an entirely new piece of the puzzle. A new layer. For the first time, I saw an opening, a portal, at a stone grouping my client called the "pig stones" on the north end of the property. Feral pigs were present in the neighborhood, as is common in Hawai'i, and my client had had a stone wall built to fence them out. I asked that the portal be closed or the energies there mitigated. Further, I asked for more clearing at the south end of the house and then special protection against the raw energies upwelling from the natural rock formation down below.

Then I saw that the "pig stones" and the area beneath the master bedroom were connected energetically (and perhaps physically?) underground. A whole realm existed there, the domain of a LowerWorld being. I talked with this being but quickly realized my client needed to talk with him directly, to come to agreement about living together in peace and comfort in their respective spaces. I asked her to sit in meditation, make the connection (I knew she was capable), and partner with the land for that aspect of the work. In certain shamanic traditions, the boar is the keeper of the LowerWorld, and the connection on this land between physical and energetic pigs was intriguing.

Even after the second session, issues remained. Progress and improvements were great as far as they went, but didn't constitute harmony. My client remained as unsettled as the land, and it began to strike me that something inherent in her needed to keep "stirring the pot."

At that point, I ended my involvement. My team and I could do no more for this particular situation. In my parting email, I recommended that she and her husband consider selling and moving if they were serious about finding simpler, more peaceful lives, though I knew they were likely to take their drama with them and interject it into whatever new space they inhabited, just as I knew that another owner might have an entirely different, and far more harmonious, experience on this troubled property. Whatever unresolved baggage we humans carry around with us is likely to be reflected back to us by the land complex. ⬥

When Land Work Is *Earth* Work

"One who is willing to give one's body for the Earth, and do so with love, is the only one fit to be steward of the Earth."

— Lao Tzu

What I term land whispering or land work doesn't ordinarily extend to the planetary level — that is, the land complex isn't ordinarily construed as *the whole Earth* or even a large part of it. But it could be. Moreover, no call to the planetary level has ever come to me through a human client. But it might.

For land work at the larger level, I use the term "Earth work." I consider this a separate but related calling and conduct it as a separate but related practice. In a way, the distinction is artificial as land is land no matter its size and complexity. The two practices are closely allied, requiring the same basic understandings and a similar skill set, and there are overlap and feedback between them in that healing any part of the land complex, no matter how localized, contributes to healing the whole, and vice versa.

But Earth work focuses on issues relating to planetary evolution, which is beyond the purview of land whispering, and beyond the scope of this book.[15] It also requires access to deeper sources, affording a deeper level of information. I use the word "deeper" advisedly as, once again, language bumps up against its limits here.

I never consciously chose to be an Earth worker anymore than I chose to be a land whisperer, though in hindsight I can see I had been training unawares for some years. In both cases, a higher authority tapped me; my only choice was to acquiesce or not.[16] I could not have conceived of the nature of Earth work until I began accepting assignments, trusting (as I also do as a land whisperer) that the appropriate energies would align at the right moment for the right purpose and that I would be guided wisely. Doing Earth work isn't regular, or at least it hasn't been for me — it comes in bursts — and I have to pay attention to the subtle signs Nature employs to know when I'm being called for the next round.

---

[15] I've written about Earth work elsewhere: See *The Shards* and *Earth Work Journal* on my website www.handonthecavewall.net. The two stories in this chapter are excerpted in slightly revised form from *The Shards*.

[16] I have always said "yes" when tapped. I don't know what happens if you say "no."

The following two stories reflect aspects of Earth work and are just a small sampler from a practice with a grand scope. The first, from my early days, recounts a shamanic journey in which I met with the Deep Ancestors, who long ago dreamed the Earth into being through their unified intention; this is one of the most powerful journeys I have ever experienced. The second, from several years later, illustrates both the intuitive and analytical nature of partnering with the elements at the planetary level.

Earth work has made clear to me how vibrantly alive and communicative our planet is, and how crucial it is that we humans take our partnership with Nature seriously.

Meeting with the Deep Ancestors... and a Surprise Guest

WHEN I BEGAN TO CONNECT with the Energy at the Center of the Earth, I had a strange dream in which I made contact with a group of humanoid beings and asked a "woman" in the group about meeting with their leader to discuss "peace." She told me "Someone can meet with you" but didn't elaborate. Then I experienced powerful — and *profoundly different* — energies and thought later that perhaps the energetic experience had been the "meeting." Six months later I journeyed shamanically and realized afterward that the encounter in the night with the humanoid group had not been a dream at all.

The Journey: <<< I was met at the outset by Big Cat, my Deep Earth ally, who led me along a forest path till we came to a high ledge overlooking a large pool at the base of a waterfall. I proceeded to swim effortlessly up the waterfall while Big Cat remained on the ledge; at the top of the falls I continued swimming upstream till suddenly I was out of the stream and inside what I later would perceive as a small forest hut. The inside of the hut was a dim cavern-like room.

In the room was a circle of robed, hooded figures of indeterminate gender. I was unable to see their faces, or perhaps their faces were indistinct. They were silent. I stood in their midst, and one arose and handed me a spinning globe which I encircled with my arms. I knew these were the Deep Ancestors (whom I'd been introduced to before in another manner and setting) and the globe in my arms was the Earth. I was told to hold the Earth just so, and to love her and send healing with the intention of integration — disintegration has been the state of affairs on Earth for far too long. I also was told this work would be tiring, and not to overdo it. I noticed Big Cat on the periphery of the room, grinning.

After a while, an Ancestor relieved me of the spinning globe, and I thought we were done. But as I was about to leave, a very unusual being appeared in the doorway of the hut. As I looked upon "him," the Ancestors turned toward "him" as well — I heard something like a collective intake of breath. Clearly they did not expect...this arrival. (I use the masculine pronoun because this being projected male energy; gender is irrelevant.)

The being was so alien looking I found him scary, yet I knew there was nothing to fear. He appeared as an amalgam of translucent blue-tinged crystals in humanoid form. Description is difficult. The being looked slightly out of focus, perhaps because I was having trouble taking him in or because he was having trouble projecting himself in a form I could relate to or perceive at all.

The circle of Ancestors parted to allow him entry, and he walked toward me and somehow communicated that he was going to meld with me to imbue me with a kind of power I would need to do the assigned work. We merged. Afterwards, the Ancestors wanted me to lie down and rest, but I told them, no need, I was fine. Then Big Cat and I left the hut, and when I turned to look back at it — this is when I saw it as a hut — it disappeared (poof!!) into a ball of golden light. >>>

Within months I knew that the unusual crystalline being encountered in this journey was the being I "met with" in the "dream" *and a* manifestation of the Energy at the Center of the Earth. ✦

Water Speaks...with Authority!

THE ISSUE OF WATER MANAGEMENT arises at local and much larger levels — that is, as both land work and Earth work.

In August 2005 the water energies began attracting my attention through a series of mundane and arcane events whose central theme was "flooding." As is often the dynamic, taken individually each event didn't signify, but taken together they formed a pattern and sent a message.

A month later, Hurricane Katrina cut a path of water-borne destruction along the US Gulf Coast, impacting many communities but most notably the city of New Orleans. Several other named hurricanes followed in Katrina's wake, causing loss of life, property, and the illusion of safety and security.

I understood that flooding wasn't limited to water. Anything could flood, and on any level. Once the levees protecting the city burst, New Orleans was flooded not only with water but also with rage, violence, crime, bigotry, and despair. What's more, flooding isn't always negative: abundance, too, is a form of flooding. In this scenario though, water had been the prime agent, and in destroyer mode (from a human perspective), and its message came through loud and clear:

> *The Water energies are demanding a true partnership with humans. Water will no longer allow itself to be "managed" by human engineering without its input and consent. Where such old-style management persists, Water will find ways to reclaim its flow dynamics and natural space. New Orleans...was created on a huge delta; the area was developed and urbanized without any consideration given to or permission sought from Water. Humans displaced Water, and now — the tables turned — Water has displaced humans. There must be*

> *parity and respect, built upon a foundation of gratitude.*
> *(journal excerpt)*

In a post-Katrina meditation, I saw the potential for future water-based events in two different areas of the continental US where people have manipulated and (unconsciously) disrespected water. In one, a naturally dry large-population center, water has been imported through a series of dammed rivers to foster development and urbanization. This area also is prone to earthquakes; an alliance between the water and earth elements could have devastating consequences on human culture. The second area is a vast floodplain cut by three major rivers and dotted with lakes and reservoirs. Coastal lands are low lying; in some locales, the coastal zone is degrading and the sea invading. The very large underlying aquifer is rapidly being depleted through agricultural irrigation.

The teaching delivered through this meditation illuminated for me the types of situations people unwittingly create through human-centered, "power over" thinking and the actions that result — and the ways in which the land-human partnership is not honored. With climate change indisputably now in the mix, we humans disregard our agreements with Nature at our peril. ✦

Land Whispering As A Path

"In the Jewish liturgy there is a prayer called Aleinu *in which we ask that the world be soon perfected under the sovereignty of God* (l'takein olam b'malkhut Shaddai). Tikkun olam, *the perfecting or the repairing of the world, has become a major theme in modern Jewish social justice theology. It is usually expressed as an activity that must be done by humans in partnership with God. It is an important concept in light of the task ahead in environmentalism. In our ignorance and our greed, we have damaged the world and silenced many of the voices of the choir of Creation. Now we must fix it. There is no one else to repair it but us."*

— From the *Huffington Post/The Blog,* Oct 7, 2013, Rabbi Lawrence Troster, *"10 Teachings on Judaism and the Environment"*

If you're aware enough and committed enough to learn, you can become a land whisperer for the environment you steward. Anyone can. If you become adept enough, you can help other stewards by collaborating with them and their land, sharing knowledge, and deepening the practice. Some do.

But few are *called* to the work, as I have been — that is, invited to walk it *as a path*. It is an honor, and humbling, to be called, *and* a responsibility. As you'll discover for yourself if you step onto this path, much is given *and* much is expected, even demanded, by those who have bestowed the privilege.

My Story

I gravitated to this calling without consciously knowing I was doing so, though I must have been preparing for it all my life.

Hindsight is golden.

Following are highlights of my personal trajectory over the past 40 years.

In the 1980s, I began learning about subtle energy through acupuncture treatments and reading Carlos Castaneda (it was a while before I realized what Castaneda was *really* talking about). My own health issues propelled me deeper into energy medicine when I went into crisis during winter 1993-94 through a catastrophic illness that also served as teacher and initiation. With invaluable assistance from a healer-teacher who simply showed up at my front door one day because she had been instructed to, the doors of perception opened wider, and I began to search out the source of my illness and, in the process, learn how to sense and work with subtle energy. I had stepped onto the healer's path.

Then, in 1995, I came to Hawai'i. My health was still precarious, and beaching it in the subtropics sounded like good medicine. Now I know that coming to Hawai'i was a call. Originally slated to be there a year, I stayed for 19.

The Island of Hawai'i has the raw, first-chakra energy emblematic of its active volcano, Kilauea, on the slopes of massive Mauna Loa. I remember visiting Volcanoes National Park for the first time and walking on land only *two weeks old*. It was still warm and steaming. I could barely wrap my mind around that. The island spirits are a populous, demonstrative presence, influencing human affairs in palpable ways. What better training ground for a land whisperer?!

Little by little I strengthened my connections to place: the plants, animals, insects, lava, stones, soil, water, wind, clouds, sun, rain, rainbows…not to mention the myriad Unseen Ones. At first, being connected was an *idea*, something solely in my head; it grew to be a *feeling*, something in my body, in my awareness, and ultimately a *knowing*. As I evolved, I drew to me people whose orientation was aligned with my development, some of whom became important teachers and dear friends.

Once well enough, I opened a bodywork practice of my own — intuitive hands-on healing combined with Jin Shin Tara — applying what I'd learned through initiatory illness and study and continuing to learn with each client. Then, unaccountably, after several years the demand for my services started falling off; after pondering this shift for a while, I took it as a message new work was in the offing. I waited and paid attention. Soon I noted within myself greater interest as a healer in a larger and more complex scale, in a new "body": the land. This too began as a slow, evolutionary learning process, but was accelerated and expanded by the events of September 11, 2001.

So when, at breakfast one morning in 2005, David and I got to talking about his usual dog-walking routes and he told me his least favorite, an area with strong energetic imprints of violence from the ancient Hawaiian martial art of lua, stirred up fantasies of violence within him, I knew instinctively the space needed to be cleared and the impetus for our conversation was a call. This was my first "official" land whispering, chronicled earlier in my story "Warrior Spirits Take Flight."

In 2006 I formalized the practice as a service — The Land Work — and developed my first website (www.thelandwork.com). Writing this book is part of my charge and ongoing commitment. In 2011 I created my second website (www.handonthecavewall.net), a more comprehensive communications platform that includes Earth work as well.

ETHICS

Being a land whisperer requires a strong moral compass. Because energy knows no boundaries, it's incumbent upon you as a practitioner to discern the scope of the work once you're called and go forward with it *for the best and highest good of all.* That intention nullifies any hidden agendas, conscious or unconscious, and assures power is used wisely.

The following is a basic ethical code of conduct for land whispering:

- *Ask permission.* Being called gives you permission to act in your capacity as a practitioner, but there may be additional, specific issues of permission to address explicitly in a given call. For instance, if a person other than your client is involved, particularly if the person is a child, you may need to ask energetically whether this involvement is appropriate. If you're land whispering at the community level, issues of permission may come up relating to the multiple properties involved and/or sociocultural, economic, historic, or ethnic/racial layers. On occasion, permission may be needed when *nonhuman* lifeforms are involved. Once you ask, the answer may be crystal clear or a subtle feeling (comfortable = yes/okay, uncomfortable = no/not okay). If you feel uneasy about proceeding, don't, or inquire further. If you still feel uneasy, stop. If you get a no/not okay on any level, stop.

- *Discern the limits and purpose of information-gathering.* Having the capability to gather information intuitively doesn't give you license.

Ask yourself: *For what purpose* am I conducting this work? Do I *need* to know? Or do I just *want* to know? Is this about gratifying my ego or about the well-being of others? If you sense a hidden agenda, stop.

- *Hold information in confidence.* Because land whispering is healing work, your relationship with clients requires confidentiality. It can be a burden to carry confidences and difficult to resist sharing them. I've used clients' stories in this book for illustrative and teaching purposes only, and, as the "Note To Readers" up front indicates, I've masked identities of people and places to avoid breaching confidentiality.

- *Remain humble.* You are not land whispering alone. The work is collaborative: you are part of a team. Moreover, doing this work is a privilege, not a right. Taking credit, bragging, or otherwise drawing attention to yourself is an arrogance those who bestowed the privilege will not tolerate. Passing judgment or creating drama is equally unacceptable behavior.

If you act unethically, you'll find yourself stripped of power, opportunity, and stewardship. If you repeatedly violate this code of conduct, there will be karmic consequences.

WORKING WITH HUMAN CLIENTS

Land whispering is always initiated by a call that comes through human clients or directly from the land itself. And there's a timing to the call and thus the work. A potential client may express interest in, even excitement about, having you land whisper a particular environment yet not follow through by setting an appointment. It happens. That simply means it's not time, and because it's not time proceeding is pointless. The impetus and follow-through must come from the client because that signals everything is in alignment for the work to succeed. This is equally true when the land itself is the "client."

Furthermore, because land whispering is a healing practice, it is inappropriate, even unethical, for a practitioner to aggressively solicit people or "encourage" a client, or potential client, to go ahead with a scheduled appointment if that person is unsure. *The client must ask and then follow through freely.* I've advertised modestly to let the community know what I offer and have a website describing the nature of the service so that people can investigate and educate themselves. But that's the extent of self-promotion. Most of my clients have come to me not because of posted flyers or e-blasts but because someone else has used and recommended my services. Word of mouth is trustworthy — and powerful.

Following is a summary of how I work with human clients for those of you who want to pursue land whispering as a service to others. As with prior protocols laid out in this book, this one also is intended as a model, a jumping-off point; experience and experimentation will help you develop your own approach over time.

- As noted in "A Land Whisperer At Work," the client and I discuss the basic problem in person or by phone, email, or skype. We set an appointment for me to come to the property if it's local to begin the assessment, during which time we walk the site and talk in detail. If the property or client is far away, we do more of the initial assessment through discussion without a site visit; I may ask for a photo or two of the property (helpful but not required).

- I charge a set amount for the assessment-clearing package; other work may be at an hourly rate unless it naturally accompanies clearing. My rates are determined intuitively, and I adjust when a client is financially strapped and asks about a sliding scale. I take part of my fee up front if the client is new to me; otherwise I bill once the work is complete. I rarely do trades and don't recommend them unless they're a perfect fit (most aren't).

- In the case of community-level land whispering, it may be impossible to charge a fee and the work is done pro bono. The "pay," or "exchange," is at another level.

- Even if I visit the property, I always complete the assessment remotely — that is, in my session space at home — asking my team for any necessary information I wasn't given on site or through discussion.

- Once assessment is complete, I proceed with clearing or other indicated work remotely, in my session space at home. Most work requires only one session.

- I give the client an update, usually by email, after the remote session closes. I may offer session-based information, but that's case dependent, and the depth and breadth of the information vary quite a bit.

- I communicate again with the client when the entire process is complete, providing additional information, recommendations, even specific instructions, as appropriate. As noted elsewhere, I thoroughly document the case from start to finish and hold this material confidential.

Interacting with clients also affords me the chance to teach informally: to educate people more deeply about the land-human partnership and ways in which they can become more conscious stewards. When I do clearings, clients need to understand how to move forward with awareness so they don't re-establish the old patterns that were just cleared! This may involve a change in behavior or mindset. I relish this teaching aspect of land whispering as much as the energywork itself as it helps empower others.

CAVEATS

In my early days exploring Hawai'i Island — where I stepped onto this path — I felt the power of place, and that generated an excitement I wanted to share with friends and family who visited. But as I learned more about the history, heard the stories, listened to cultural practitioners, and grew in awareness, I realized it wasn't wise to expose visitors indiscriminately to the resident energies. This is true for any locale, not just Hawai'i.

Why?

Whenever you step into a new environment, you take on the energies there and add those, consciously or unconsciously, to your realm of responsibilities (in Hawaiian, your *kuleana*). If you lack the vitality, resources, awareness, or training and step into a situation unprepared, you may be harmed. People close to you may be harmed. Generally this is *not* because the energies are malicious but for other reasons; for instance, the vibrational frequencies may be more than your own system is circuited for, or the circumstances may require a level of expertise you haven't attained. When the energies *are* malicious — they can be! — the potential for harm is even greater *because of how intention colors energy*: the energy that can heal also can do damage or even kill.

I am talking here about *power* — and working with power is serious business. It is not something to play at or play with. It is not about "parlor tricks."

Individual and gender differences also must be considered. I avoid sites I know to have very dense (low frequency) energy because they nauseate me and/or create intense pressure at my temples, though they may affect another land whisperer differently or not at all. If I encounter such a site unexpectedly or am called to work on one, I minimize my exposure, getting in and out as quickly as possible, then clear and rebalance my own energy field. Shielding myself energetically before I go on site or as soon as I sense a problem may mitigate the discomfort.

In some cultures, women are prohibited from entering certain areas and participating in certain rituals not because of what we'd call sexist attitudes but as *energetic protection*. A woman's system may not be configured energetically to handle the vibrational frequencies involved.

I have not encountered the converse — that is, men being prohibited from participating because of potential harm to their energetic configuration — but it may occur.

Land whispering is a sacred trust. If you're not prepared for the responsibility, do not walk this path.

STEPPING UP

I recall working with a client with a strong intuitive gift of her own (though not as a land whisperer), one she'd been aware of since girlhood but hadn't yet developed to its fullest. At the close of my service, she thanked me not only for the work at her home but also for our intrepid conversations and my guidance about using her innate gift. I knew she felt a kinship with me and understood the relief that feeling brought. In fact, this put me in mind of my own beginnings as an energyworker years ago when I was on the steepest part of the learning curve under very difficult conditions (catastrophic illness), lacked confidence and was often bewildered by the nature of my new experiences, and needed all the support I could muster. I was, and still am, enormously grateful to my earliest teachers, and indeed to anyone I could talk to openly then without feeling "crazy."

The value of "paying it forward" — of helping those newer on the path when you yourself are farther along — cannot be overemphasized. It's what keeps these kinds of spiritual lineages vital and encourages those with gifts to *step up* — that is, not only to use the gift fully but to *take it to the next level*. And to keep stepping up at every crucial juncture when greater service is required. After all, this is why the gift was given in the first place.

Working intuitively is both an art and a craft. Much about the art is innate. Much about the craft can be learned through committed study and practice. Teachers and teachings do indeed appear when the student is ready, presenting themselves in diverse and sometimes unexpected forms. Intuitive gifts are not parceled out gratuitously. Each recipient has been not only granted the *privilege* but also tasked with both *purpose* and *responsibility*. Said another way: To whom much is given, much is expected.

Stepping up is *transformative*. Often it is *initiatory*. It may be inconvenient, life-altering in startling ways, painful, upending. There may be major shifts in life circumstances: you may lose friends, your job, your partner, your living situation. You may lose your health for a time. But whatever is lost in one sector, at one level, will be gained in another, and within the challenges lies the opportunity to step *up* and *into* the life you were born for.

IN MY WORLD...

"May the Earth become one with the soles of your feet and keep you firm, may it sustain your body when it loses its balance. May the wind cool your ears and offer you at any hour the answers that will heal all that your anguish might invent. May the fire nourish your gaze and purify the victuals that will feed your soul. May the rain be your ally, may it offer you its caresses, cleanse your body and mind of all that does not belong to you."

— Grandmother blessing her granddaughter, from *Malinche,* by Laura Esquivel, 2006, Atria Books, NY

What if we *live* the truths put forward in this book? That we're related and connected to all other beings. That other beings are intelligent, and communicating with them is as basic as breathing. That the most fundamental nature of our environment is *energetic*, and its condition matters because it shapes our thoughts, feelings, and actions.

Here's a glimpse of how things work in a more highly evolved world… what I like to call *my world*.

> *In my world*, every time land changes hands, it's energetically assessed and cleared to release old patterns of disharmony and attract more aware stewards. Land work is part of the sale protocol for realtors, part of the rental protocol for property managers.
>
> *In my world*, homes are cleared annually to release the energetic debris of relationships and family dynamics. Workplaces are cleared once or twice a year, more frequently if they're large spaces filled daily with scores of customers. Cleared environments are more comfortable for employees and more pleasing to clientele, all of which benefits commerce.
>
> *In my world*, subtle-energy basics are taught at home by aware parents along with everything else parents teach. Energy basics are taught in schools as *language* — the proto-language, the lingua franca, of sentient life. They're taught as *science* — given the right technology, physicists may one day be able to measure or mathematically describe the set of vibrational frequencies constituting subtle energy. Subtle-energy basics are taught as mainstream, not "complementary" or "alternative," *medicine*. They're taught as *philosophy* — the energetic templates of material reality are akin to Plato's Realm of Forms.
>
> *In my world*, cropland, rangeland, and managed forests are assessed for the state of their health and cleared of imbalances, also benefiting productivity. Waterways and bodies of water are assessed and treated appropriately, as are wild lands. Municipalities

take into account land-human partnership agreements and the power of all four elements in their urban design and planning.

In my world, land work is routine for public spaces like libraries, schools, airports, courthouses, other government buildings — the list is long — to transmute the energetic human detritus that accumulates there through the course of daily interactions. Hospitals, doctors' offices, and veterinary clinics are cleared of the stress and pathology of illness. Prisons and jails are cleared of the underlying patterns of violence held by both inmates and corrections officers. Neighborhoods prone to crime are cleared of those vibrations to improve their social health.

In my world, areas that are or have been war zones, battlefields, and terrorist targets are cleared to release trauma, shock, and pain from the space. Shifting the energetic baseline makes those areas less likely to attract more violence. The spirits of those killed, both combatants and civilians, are assisted where they're confused and unable to transition on their own.

In my world, cemeteries are assessed energetically to assure the spirits are at peace. Spirits who haven't fully transitioned are helped on their journey, and any lingering negative residues around the deaths of those buried there and the grief of those left behind are cleared.

In my world, land whispering comes out of the closet, and we practitioners take our rightful place in the community.

Today, *my world* is just a thought-world. But thoughts are powerful. Tomorrow it may be *your* world. *Our* world.

Glossary

ALL OUR RELATIONS: A phrase often used by indigenous people to refer to the great web of life, all of which is considered *connected and animate*. Any of these relations may be called *brother, sister, aunty, uncle, cousin, grandmother, grandfather*, and so on to reinforce this understanding.

ANIMATE: All inspirited forms; that is, all forms imbued with life-force and energy.

ASSESSMENT: The diagnostic process of sensing the condition of the land complex on a given site once you've been called there as a land whisperer; assessment may be done on site, remotely, or a combination of the two and may be general or detailed.

BATTLE ENERGY: Energetic imprints within the space of a battlefield or war zone; I first became aware of this term in *Universal Light Series 2*, a publication of the Perelandra Center for Nature Research, and now apply it more broadly to any energy of violence or conflict.

CALL: The energetic communiqué from a given site to a land whisperer; the call may come directly from the land or may be framed as a "problem" by a human client.

CLEARING: The process through which disharmonious energies and energy patterns, often old and multilayered, are gently released from a given space and transmuted; most of the work I'm called to do involves clearing. Clearing can be a one-time event or periodic energetic "housekeeping."

DARK ENERGIES: Power distortions sourcing from the unhealed self; dark energies feed on negativity and can cause harm. Whenever dark energies may be involved in land whispering, I ask for extra protection as a precaution.

DEEP ANCESTORS: Those who dreamed the Earth into being through their unified intention. For more information, see *The Shards* in www.handonthecavewall.net.

DENSE ENERGY: Old, stagnant energy that concentrates over time, especially on sites that need to be cleared; may also be lower frequency energy.

DIMENSION: A world characterized by a certain range of vibrational frequencies; the Universe comprises multiple dimensions.

DISCERNMENT: The finely balanced marriage of intuition and intellect, crucial to properly interpreting the raw data perceived in land whispering

DIVINATION (or INTUITIVE MIRRORING): A technique for projecting unconscious information onto an external "screen" so you can "read" it. Formal systems include tarot, I Ching, runes, and palmistry, but almost anything can serve as an intuitive mirror.

ELEMENTS: Fire, water, earth, and air.

ENERGETIC IMPRINT: Residual subtle energy or energetic pattern in an environment.

ENERGY: See SUBTLE ENERGY.

EX-HUMANS: A spirit formerly in a human body, often an on-site guardian. See also GUARDIAN SPIRITS.

GATE (or GATEWAY): An extremely powerful, significant node in the Earth's energetic grid.

GREAT SISTERS: In Hawai'i, the deities Pele and Poliahu. Pele is the goddess of fire and volcanoes and is also known as Grandmother Earth; her home is Kilauea volcano, on the shoulder of massive Mauna Loa. Poliahu is the goddess of ice and snow, her home Mauna Kea, the tallest mountain on Earth from the seafloor and considered by many as the most sacred mountain in Polynesia. See also UNIVERSAL ENERGIES.

GREMLINS: Spirits who often play "pranks" to get humans' attention to redress an issue on site; usually not harmful.

GUARDIAN SPIRITS: Ex-humans or other beings who choose to remain on site as caretaker-protectors, sometimes for long periods, because of their love of place or a responsibility conferred on them by those unknown or unknowable; guardian spirits may eventually come to the end of their term and seek the help of a land whisperer to exit. See TRANSITION.

GUIDANCE: Higher level wisdom.

INTERDIMENSIONAL TEAM or I-TEAM: The council of beings I partner with to land whisper a site; some team members are a core group involved with every call, others site- or situation-specific.

INTUITIVE MIRRORING: See DIVINATION.

KINESIOLOGY (or MUSCLE TESTING): A simple technique that uses the body's electrical system to give information in response to yes-or-no questions.

LAND or LAND COMPLEX: The space comprising all physical/material lifeforms, elements, spirit-beings, and structures residing upon, within, or above a piece of ground of any size and usage. The land is a container of energy, form, relationship, and interaction.

LAND WHISPERER or LAND WORKER: A healer who communicates and partners energetically with a given environment to assure or restore balance.

LIFEFORMS: Participants in the land-human partnership; all who are animate.

"LIKE ATTRACTS LIKE": The positive feedback loop in which a particular energy, issue, or pattern attracts more of the same, reinforcing the loop (cycle). If the loop is undesirable, energetic clearing can be used to break the cycle.

LOST SPIRITS/SOULS: Beings who are unaware of their associated physical body's death, confused about their situation, and unable to transition without help. Sometimes encountered in land whispering.

LOWERWORLD: One of three interconnected realms — UpperWorld, MiddleWorld, and LowerWorld — in classical shamanic tradition. The three realms and their central axis, the World Tree, appear in one form or another in many human cultures.

MALE/FEMALE ENERGIES: The two fundamental, complementary, and (when in balance) harmonious aspects of all life. Everything has a male and female aspect regardless of gender or lifeform, as these are energies with associated qualities.

MUSCLE TESTING: See KINESIOLOGY.

NATURE: Universal intelligence; the great family of vibrational frequencies emanating from the origin of the Universe.

PIPELINE: An energetic pathway containing many spirit-beings, often part of a multidimensional network.

PORTAL: An energetic opening or doorway into other dimensions or worlds, allowing beings to move between them.

REMOTELY/REMOTE WORK: Doing land whispering while *not* physically on the site being treated; assessment, clearing, and other processes all may be done through intention any distance from a given environment.

SENSING BODY: The intuitive aspect of our human nature; not a discrete body but a layer of consciousness. See also THINKING BODY.

SHAMANIC JOURNEY: An ancient practice in many world cultures in which the energyworker shifts consciousness through drumming or another sound source and enters other worlds for information and healing for others.

SHIELDING: An energetic technique used to create a protective buffer around a person, other being, or place. A shield is not a wall but a filter that mitigates energetic impact.

SPIRIT: See SOUL.

SPIRIT NATION or THE UNSEEN ONES: The vast, complex array of spirit-beings who populate the world, sensed energetically and partnered with in land whispering.

SPIRITS OF PLACE: The particular set of energies and beings belonging to a place. They have responsibilities to that place and are essential land-whispering partners.

SOUL: The spirit essence inhabiting physical lifeforms, including the aggregate of the land complex itself. In some cultures, the soul has multiple aspects with different names and other attributes. In this book *soul* is used as a general term and is sometimes interchangeable with *spirit*.

SOUL RETRIEVAL: In land whispering, the process of calling back the lost soul or soul pieces of the land.

SOUL TRANSITION: The process of a soul moving beyond the 3rd dimension once the associated physical body has died. May also be referred to as SOUL RELEASE.

SUBTLE ENERGY: The substrate of all life regardless of dimension.

SUBTLE SENSES: Nonphysical senses through which we intuit and perceive beyond the 3rd dimension.

SUBTLE WORLD: The aggregate of all energetic flows, forms, imprints, and templates.

THE UNSEEN ONES: See SPIRIT NATION.

THINKING BODY: The intellectual, or mental, aspect of our human nature; not a discrete body but a layer of consciousness. See also SENSING BODY.

TRANSECT: A line of energy.

TRANSITION: Move from one energetic level or plane to another.

TRANSMUTE: Shift energies to a higher level or plane.

TRAPPED SPIRITS/SOULS: Beings who, for whatever reason, are stuck in the Earth plane after their physical bodies have died and are unable to transition without help. Sometimes encountered in land whispering.

UNIVERSAL ENERGIES: Powerful spirit-beings whose domain is planetary and beyond. They include the four elements under a variety of names and guises, cultural archetypes, enlightened ones, sleepers and redeemers, and others who may be unknown to us or even unknowable.

Acknowledgments

I am grateful to all my relations.

Of those I've known personally who've supported the work and my evolution as a land whisperer, I thank

David A. Perry Sr., my husband of 32 years and shamanic partner.

Rachel Cook Carpenter, Raylene Ha'alelea Kawaiae'a, Tom Grunden (Anahata), Uncle Ed Stevens, and Hilton Nalani Cabrera.

Gretchen Bracher, Eve Llyndorah, Elaine Christianson, Genevieve Firestone, and Kepaniwai (Brian Devine).

Jan Ellison, Michál Carrillo, Joel and Michelle Levey, Susan Caravalho, and Mary Frazier.

Nicole Becker, Gloria Schliesser, Kunzang Roesler, and Afia Walking Tree for the "lighthouse."

Bonnie Iki and Hala for their companionship and teachings.

WavenDean Fernandes for the term "land whisperer."

For their masterful work as I've come to know it through their writing, I thank

Carlos Castaneda, Machaelle Small Wright, R.J. Stewart, Caitlín Matthews, Eliot Pattison, and Barry Holstun Lopez.

For their artistry in bringing this book into form, I thank

Margaret Copeland for the thoughtful, elegant design that honors the nature of the content and practice; and Eve Llyndorah for the luminous, otherworldly painting so generously offered to grace the cover and serve as a presentiment of what lies within.

Finally, and inevitably, I thank

Hawai'i Nei, the transformative space whose energies and forces ushered me, with intention, into land whispering.

All my clients, including the land itself.

My teachers in their myriad forms.

The Unseen Ones who tapped me for this work.

My i-teams, without whom land whispering is impossible.

About The Author

CAROL ROSENBLUM PERRY is a land and Earth worker by calling (since 2001) and an editor-writer by profession (since 1978). A New Yorker by birth, she has lived in Oregon and Hawai'i and now makes her home in the San Francisco Bay Area.

Land Whisperer / A Guide to Partnering Energetically with Any Environment is her second book. Her book *The Fine Art of Technical Writing*, in print since 1991 and the capstone to her editing career at Oregon State University, remains a writer's worthy companion. She is currently at work on *Ruby and Vera Dreaming*, a novel for young adults.